GENDER OUTLAWS

THE NEXT GENERATION

KATE BORNSTEIN

and

S. BEAR BERGMAN

SEAL PRESS

GENDER OUTLAWS
The Next Generation

Copyright © 2010 by Kate Bornstein and S. Bear Bergman

Published by
Seal Press
A Member of the Perseus Books Group
1700 Fourth Street
Berkeley, California

Library of Congress Cataloging-in-Publication Data

Gender outlaws : the next generation / edited by Kate Bornstein and S.
Bear Bergman.
    p. cm.
  ISBN 978-1-58005-308-2
  1. Transsexuals—Identity. 2. Gender identity. 3. Sex change. 4. Sex
(Psychology) I. Bornstein, Kate, 1948- II. Bergman, S. Bear, 1974-
  HQ77.9.G39 2010
  306.76'8—dc22

                                    2010010372

Cover design by Kimberly Glyder
Cover Illustration by Candace Sepulis
Interior design by Domini Dragoone
Printed in the United States of America by LSC Communications
Distributed by Publishers Group West

To Stanley Safran Bergman,
the next generation

CONTENTS

Introduction

Kate Bornstein and S. Bear Bergman

AIM IM 3/9/10 11:01 AM

S. Bear Bergman: Good morning, cutepants.

Kate Bornstein: What a perfectly delightful way to open a conversation.

SBB: It's easy to be delightful when one is delighted, in my experience.

KB: Now see, this is like the old days.

SBB: ::laughing:: It is, in fact. I went digging through old files in preparation for this chat, and we evidently used to have a lot of spare time to spend flirting.

KB: Next generation, huh? I have a serious typing thing that I do: when I try to type generation, it ALWAYS comes out genderation. I did it just now.

SBB: You're not alone in that, it seems. After I started forwarding the call for submissions for *GO:TNG*, a lot of the replies with submissions attached came to *Gender Outlaws: The Next Genderation*.

KB: Really? It just wants to come out my fingers like that.

SBB: Muscle memory?

KB: More like inner vaudevillian.

SBB: ::laughing:: I've never really thought of your vaudevillian as "inner," exactly, but okay.

SBB: If I'd been a different sort of a being, I might have taken up burlesque.

KB: As would I, my darling. And we'd do a double act and wow the crowds.

SBB: Yes, indeed.

KB: So what year did you and I meet?

SBB: I think 1993.

KB: Holy poop, 1993?

SBB: The oldest files of email I have are from 1994, and they seem clear that we'd already met in person. And they're from spring. So I think we met in person sometime in 1993. 17 years, give or take.

KB: ::shaking my head::

SBB: If our friendship were a person, it would be a college freshman by now.

KB: And you were how old? I shudder to re-ask.

SBB: In 1993? I would have been 18 or 19. But I was precocious.

KB: You were more than precocious.

SBB: I was looking for a kinder word than "insufferable know-it-all."

KB: That too, but you made it charming.

SBB: ::laughing:: Well, thank g-d for that.

SBB: I think we got to be friends just as the original *Gender Outlaw* was kind of hitting its stride, though. I remember you were suddenly touring more, and that to some degree we bonded over being pervs and Macintosh enthusiasts.

KB: Days of Gwen Smith's Gazebo, and my twice-weekly *Star Trek* text-based games in AOL chatrooms.

KB: That's right, 'cuz I was carrying my Mac Classic around with me on my back in the special convenient backpack Apple made for it.

SBB: Yep, and you logged on from everywhere—the first person I knew who did. But it really is, actually . . . wait, how long is a generation, technically?

KB: Length of time between end of the original series and beginning of the next gen series. Hang on, I'll check.

SBB: ::laughing::

KB: TNG premiered 21 years after TOS.

KB: 1987, my first year of womanhood. A lot more happens to a generation of queers in much shorter time. The cultural version of epigenetics, where evolution of a species is proved to have noticeably jumped in just one generation.

SBB: I feel like, by the time I knew you, you were already saying a lot about how gender wasn't what most of us thought.

SBB: ::quietly googles "epigenetics"::

SBB: How do you feel about where this "genderation" is starting, as opposed to where you started?

KB: In a word, thrilled. In more than a word, awed by the heights from which this gen of gender outlaws has leapt off into their unexplored spaces. People today are STARTING from further than I got to when I'd finished writing *Gender Outlaw*. That's EXACTLY what I hoped to live to see.

SBB: And I think part of why is because you *did* write *Gender Outlaw*. I see a direct link. I feel like I can easily trace a line through from the people I know who are roughly your age, or roughly your age-queer, through my cohort, and to the place where people who are just moving into the fullness of themselves are now.

KB: A lot was going on when *Gender Outlaw* came out. *GO* was the piece that went furthest into the academy. But the politics of transfolk were jumping by leaps and bounds.

SBB: There was a . . . kickstart? I am not sure I was as aware of it at the time. But I definitely *saw* trans-identified people for the first time, starting then.

KB: And it was mostly trans women who were leading the cultural charge. Today, the sitch is reversed: the cultural icon for transgender is young FTM, evolved from middle-aged MTF. That bit of evolution in just one genderation.

SBB: I always wonder why that is.

KB: Kickstart was *Stone Butch Blues*.

SBB: Published in 1993.

KB: All the queens died in the '80s, and Kings took up their tiaras. Lou Sullivan wrote his words in the late '80s. When was *Gender Outlaw* first published?

SBB: I would have said the same year, but Wikipedia tells me a year later: *Stone Butch Blues* in spring of 1993, and then *Gender Outlaw* in spring of 1994.

SBB: *Stone Butch Blues* hit me like a truck. I probably read the entire book four times in a row before I could even consider picking up another book.

KB: I read it twice through on the first go, several times shortly afterwards. I know how deeply it spoke to FTMs and butches, but it spoke as deeply to femmes. At least it did to me. *Stone Butch Blues* taught me there would be butch women who would like freaky girly me. I'd met some butch women before that, and yeah they were gallant and breath-taking. But until *Stone Butch Blues*, I thought they were the exceptions.

SBB: Sometimes I have this odd, split-brain thing about the impact of the AIDS pandemic. My visceral memory is of the second wave of deaths, the early '90s, when I was chaining myself to things with ACT UP and dying-in with Queer Nation. But then I don't think about or talk about it in relation to trans politics. I think there's some sort of sanitized corner of my brain that is afraid if I talk about it, people will carry on thinking all transpeople are MTF street-involved sex workers with AIDS.

KB: For a long time, when I was coming out, the MTFs were in fact street-involved sex workers with AIDS. Two of my dear friends died the year I stepped through the looking-glass.

KB: The butch-femme dance then was gallant and gracious. That's the part of you that I responded to most quickly and deeply: the gallantry of you, the gentleman-ness.

SBB: The reverse thing was also happening for me. It was the perfect time to come out as a young butch. There were all these fantastic, hot, brilliant femmes who were so keen to help me refine and magnify my butch gallantry.

KB: Now see, I didn't meet femmes until later when I moved to Seattle. SF in those days was still Birkenstocks and plaid shirted lesbians who wanted nothing to do with men in dresses.

SBB: I learned how to do it, largely, by folding myself around the desires of the femmes I knew, like you, who loved the performativity of femme and taught me through it.

KB: You were SO attentive. Yes. Still are.

SBB: I felt seen for the first time. I felt . . . real, for the first time.

SBB: As though there was, fucking finally, a good *reason* I was like I was. It was the parable of the ugly ducking all over again. Though I wouldn't really compare myself to a swan, except for how noisy they are.

KB: and all that poop? ::ducking::

SBB: ::grin:: That too.

SBB: And you were, always have been, still are, one of my favorite flirt-partners, because you're also performative, and shape-shifting, and so . . . whimsical. So playful.

KB: Did you first feel that real-ness online or in-person?

SBB: Online.

SBB: Absolutely.

SBB: I translated it into my in-person life. Not without some hiccups, mind you. But eventually.

KB: Re: flirting, performance, and shape-shifting—sweetest of gentle creatures that you are—you KNOW it takes one to know one. We were teaching each other, and yeah that's how I learned to put that flirt energy into my offline life.

KB: Many hiccups.

SBB: Yes, many hiccups.

KB: The ouch is always gonna be there for outlaws.

SBB: Also, it turns out that when you learn some of your flirting skills from bathhouse fags, a certain . . . muting is required before trying them on college girls. Jes' sayin.

KB: hahahahahahahaha!

SBB: ::rueful smile::

KB: Even this new generation. They're starting with more, so the ouches are bigger. Higher stakes.

SBB: Because we don't get to practice our identities in junior high, when everyone else is also a fumbling idiot. We're busy trying to survive the bully culture, as you term it.

KB: It's not a simple case of "Gee, we have it so much better off than the old days of trans-dom."

SBB: No. And sometimes the ouches come from older transfolk who don't like seeing the binary they invested in get dumped out and turned into a hat by nineteen-year-olds.

KB: That's 'cuz yes, there's a new genderation, but it's not like EVERYONE is part of it. There's always gonna be transfolk entering the spectrum at the point I entered it back in the '80s. And 20 years from now, those folks are gonna be landing in the territory today's new generation has staked out. Can't fucking WAIT to see our grandkids, your son Stanley's gen.

SBB: That cartoon in the book, by Roe-Anne Alexander, where the last panel shows a kilted, lipsticked, bi-hawked young person saying "In twenty years all your kids will look like me"? I love that idea.

SBB: (Though please remind me of that the first time Stanley comes home with a surprise piercing, will you?)

KB: It's not gonna be a piercing that Stanley surprises you with, that's for sure.

SBB: Do you also spend a lot of time wondering how or why some people bust out into the new genderation, and some don't? I really think about that a lot—and how race affects it, and class.

SBB: And especially, what it means to look like a freak. And does that create freedom, or require it, or both?

KB: And citizenship and religion and all the other cultural forces and vectors of oppression that forge gender and sexuality.

KB: More please on your last question.

SBB: Okay. So I know some people who have so many skills, or so much money, or so much talent that they can almost be as freaky-looking or as gender-adjacent or whatever as they want, and they will still be fine—still able to eat and support themselves, still able to move in the world, still able to attract company and friends and lovers.

SBB: They have so much freedom because of some *other* place of privilege that they get extra slack.

SBB: But I also know people whose innate, insistent need to be exactly as they are has trumped even their need to preserve a survival strategy in terms of employment. They have ended up kind of busting up through the sidewalk, regardless.

SBB: And I don't mean to set those up as a binary, either. I am mostly just noodling around a lot, recently, in the questions of from which directions the pressure is generated and how it affects the results.

KB: Yes, and on the other side of the binary you don't mean to set up (but you don't have to set up 'cuz it really is there), there will always be *more* people who, given the same privilege, are gonna use it to wall themselves off and/or blend themselves into the culture that would otherwise call them freaks. There's a heart factor, a spirit factor that allows for the privilege to be used as a diving board into the depths of a culture.

SBB: I love that image.

KB: At its best, it's the concept of Bodhisattva: the conscious decision to re-incarnate as a lower and lower life-form lifetime after lifetime so that when you finally do attain enlightenment, the radiance will reach all sentient beings everywhere. Apply that to one lifetime, and that's what we do. At our noblest.

SBB: Whoa.

KB: Yeah. Who knew, right?

SBB: And when we say lower, we mean less powerful, less privileged?

KB: Give the gentleman a kewpie doll.

KB: It's the only way I can justify using what privilege I've got.

SBB: ::nod:: I hear that. For sure. And I'm glad we have some conversation about privilege in the book.

SBB: Though there was a lot more conversation about it outside the book. I don't know if we want to go there, but there was that entire argument that didn't make it into the book. Nobody wrote about it. . . .

KB: . . . do go on, please

SBB: Well, we used the word *tranny* in the call for submissions. And some people got very angry about that, and equated it with words of racist hate speech, and demanded that we remove it because it's a word that has been used to denigrate transpeople, especially transfeminine-spectrum people.

SBB: It felt really a lot like the arguments about Queer Nation, twenty years ago.

KB: Nice analogy

SBB: It did feel just exactly like when I was sixteen and being all Queer National and I would get *screamed* at—by gays!—for wearing a t-shirt identifying myself as queer, and being overtly sexual. In both cases I was told I had set "the movement" back twenty years.

SBB: Hey—twenty years. A whole generation. ::lightbulb goes on::

KB: Go for it

SBB: I'm going to get in trouble again.

KB: Mama lion is here to watch out for you, cub.

SBB: But many of the people, in both cases, who were so angry with me seemed to be people one generation older than I was. And maybe their fear of those words was too visceral to move past, you know? But it's as though all of those folks, having finally attained for themselves a little scrap of privilege, were just determined to protect it—even against me. Maybe especially against me. There was a real little surge of people just so excited to mention everything I have ever done wrong in my entire life which—as you know—is plenty of things.

KB: Yes, yes, yes. What I was saying about co-existing generations. The people angry with you are the same people who threw me out of a trans-sexual support group I co-founded in Philly in the mid-80s. They said I wasn't a real transsexual 'cuz I was a lesbian. All of us have held on to some precarious ledge of social decency. Some of us let go and fall into outlaw territory, others drag themselves up to cultural approbation.

KB: Queer was a homophobic slur before queers took it on as a badge of honor, but tranny was the other way round. I was using the word tranny way before it made it into the culture as a racist slur. So were you. It was a fun word we used for ourselves. Dominant culture always manages to steal and pervert those words, i.e. "It's so gay."

KB: Tranny was a word the US imported from the most fab drag culture in the world: Sydney Australia. The queens and the transsexuals (all MTF) hung out with each other. They both looked down on each other to be sure, but they knew they were family so they co-owned the word tranny. Originally, the word was used in the spirit of family. That's how I use it now. Fuck anyone who uses it as a slur.

SBB: Which, by the way, I do not see gays gathering together and trying to outlaw.

KB: Some gay folks are trying to outlaw "it's so gay." It's keeping them back from social acceptability.

SBB: I can see the argument for outlawing "it's so gay" better. They're trying to outlaw bullying, but "don't be mean" isn't—evidently—an enforceable school rule, so they list particular meannesses the young people are not permitted to engage in.

KB: But look at what happened a generation after people were damning the word queer. Now, it's something you can major in, in college.

SBB: Do you ever fantasize about how things would be if you were Queen of the World, and who you would put in charge of things. If I were King, I would love to put you in charge of shoes, gadgets, and junior high schools.

KB: ::nodding:: I'd take that from ya, yer kingship. Someone came up with a great identity on Twitter a couple of weeks ago: Warrior jester. That's what I wanna be. That and diesel femme.

KB: We need LOOKS studies, for sure. That's what it's gonna grow into.

SBB: Probably. Do you think we'll get Women's, Gender, and Tranny Studies?

KB: No, but we might somewhere get Queer and Tranny Studies.

SBB: I would like that.

KB: Me too. Someone who's reading this book is gonna make that happen.

SBB: The think I just thought is: people are who are super-protective to police the word tranny have no real confidence in the cultural power of transpeople. They police it because they fear that if not-trans-identified people get hold of it, their power will make it always and forever a *bad* word. And I, we, feel fine about it because we have a lot of faith in the cultural power of transfolks—of trannies—to make and be change.

KB: Smart you thinking the thought you just thought.

SBB: That feels like the crux of it to me, finally. Not even about their own privilege so much as fear.

KB: And the cool thing is that this book is full of people who disagree on a lot of theory but they all have faith in the cultural power of trannies to make and be change.

SBB: Yes. In fact, we may well have selected along that theme without even being able to articulate that yet.

SBB: But we definitely chose work from people who were looking forward, with their tools in their hands.

KB: Yeah. For a while, I thought the criteria was "hopeful for the future," but that's not the case in every piece in this book. Many entries in here are bleak and scary. But every single one of 'em keeps moving forward with their lives. Every single one of 'em, I admire for that.

SBB: And they also show us some portion of what it takes to do that. What they draw on for strength or inspiration, or how they imagine themselves into a really uncertain future.

KB: (I am partial to the sexy make-you-laugh-gasp-cry pieces though)

SBB: There are certainly some of those—even one with pictures.

KB: And that's a HUGE stride forward in this next generation. Why, in my day. . . .

KB: ::stroking long, white beard::

SBB: ::pulls up a stool next to your armchair::

SBB: ::leans my head toward you, face shining::

KB: In my day, we weren't allowed to associate sexy with trans because in the eyes of the dominant culture, sexy diminished the value, import, and significance of the trans experience.

KB: ::patting your sweet upturned cheek::

SBB: I think people are still being punished for being trans and sexy, for wanting to be desirable. For having the temerity not to just be quietly grateful for anyone's sexual attentions, but to insist that people learn about our bodies, learn how to touch us and talk about us. Which is why I'm so glad to have gotten the hott submissions we did, and were able to publish.

KB: Sexy is one step below tranny, something that respectable transfolk can look down on. So the fact that this next gen of gender outlaws has leapt merrily into sexy is that Boddhisatva version of lower, meaning less powerful, less privileged . . . more radiant.

KB: We have an excellent hott quotient in this book, yes. Would have been dreadful without that.

SBB: And a fairly satisfying amount of crankiness.

KB: Queer theory only works side by side with queer practice, otherwise queer theory is straight.

KB: Cranky. Ah yes, at my age I walk the fine line between crone and curmudgeon.

KB: CUTE crone.

KB: CUTE curmudgeon.

SBB: I love that transpeople are now at a place, culturally, where we're not just quietly grateful for being allowed to live. Some of the essays in this book reflect people's righteously cranky reflections on gender politics. That feels new, and totally important.

KB: That IS new, IS totally important.

SBB: You know I have always had a curmudgeon fetish.

KB: ::making a note::

KB: Ogod, I just had this picture of you and Andy Rooney. Noooooooooooo oooooooooooooooooooooo!

SBB: I think because I see my own curmudgeonliness in the not-so-distant future.

SBB: Oh, dear.

SBB: How about me and Clint Eastwood?

SBB: Wait—is he a Republican?

KB: Nooooooooooooooooooooooooooo!

SBB: You wouldn't watch me fuck Clint Eastwood?

KB: Ok, I'd watch that.

SBB: ::grin:: Phew.

KB: But I don't like his politix.

SBB: Maybe I can introduce him to a new spirit of openness.

KB: Is this where I ask you if you'd watch me fuck Sarah Palin?

SBB: One of my lovers has the idea that all world leaders should be fucked up the ass on a regular schedule, to promote flexibility and compassion.

SBB: Oh, honey. Sarah Palin? She does not deserve that.

KB: "One of your lovers." You say it so casually. Poly is a HUGE leap forward for this next gen of outlaws.

KB: She not only deserves it, she'll get it any time she asks for it.

KB: I bet Sarah Palin tastes good. All that moose for dinner.

SBB: Well, I think because there's a previous generation of gender outlaws whose refrain—from the doctors of the university system—was "keep quiet, or no one will ever want you, and maybe not even if you do." But then we had this—

SBB: oh, you're killing me with this.

SBB: ::squick::

KB: purrrrrrrrrrrrrrr

SBB: Ahem.

KB: I NEVER envisioned schools actually teaching *Gender Outlaw*. I wrote it for people who wanted to study it from a different point of view, but never thought it would catch on like it has. Eerie. David Harrison predicted it'd take off the way it did.

SBB: As I was saying. There are certain bad grrl smartypants tranny sexpot authors who really went about seeding the idea that it was okay to be sexy, and I think transfolk started to embrace a more . . . abundant idea about what relationships could look like. From there, poly was a short step.

SBB: Your books are taught in hundreds of universities. You pack rooms when you lecture about gender, and what it's not and never has been. That's always been my experience, or one of my experiences, of transgender.

KB: ::reaching down, lifting your chin up to bring your eyes to mine:: You are a very good bad boy.

SBB: ::grinning right up into your eyes:: Why thank you, ma'am. I do try.

KB: I know re: yours and others' experience of your generation. And that's WEIRD!

KB: All I wanted to do was be pretty.

KB: Really.

KB: Honest.

SBB: I know. But you know how that authenticity thing works. It draws people like nothing else in the world. It certainly drew me.

KB: Oh, so you're not bad . . . you're just drawn that way? ::ducking::

SBB: ::nods solemnly::

KB: I want you to know I'm being very good in not writing down all the thoughts I'm still having about me and Sarah Palin out on some Pacific Northwest island. Ogodogodogod.

SBB: But seriously—my early experiences of trans-anything were you, or Les Feinberg, both wicked smart and nine kinds of hot, standing at the front of the room, respectfully introduced by a university professor to waves of applause. It gave me, and people my age-queer, a kind of freedom that was unprecedented.

SBB: I never felt like being trans was The End Of The World.

KB: Agreed.

SBB: And there are a lot more people who agree with us than there used to be. Look:

Do I *look* like an outlaw to you?

Part One

We're All Someone's Freak

Gwendolyn Ann Smith

Being transgender guarantees you will upset someone. People get upset with transgender people who choose to inhabit a third gender space rather than "pick a side." Some get upset at transgender people who do not eschew their birth histories. Others get up in arms with those who opted out of surgical options, instead living with their original equipment. Ire is raised at those who transition, then transition again when they decide that their initial change was not the right answer for them. Heck, some get their dander up simply because this or that transgender person simply is not "trying hard enough" to be a particular gender, whatever that means. Some are irked that the Logo program *RuPaul's Drag Race* shows a version of transgender life different from their own. Meanwhile, all around are those who have decided they aren't comfortable with the lot of us, because we dared to change from one gender expression or identity to some other.

To hell with that.

You see, I have learned not only that I have to do what I have to do to be happy regardless of the struggles I may face, but also that I am the only person responsible for my own comfort or discomfort about my gender. I may wrinkle my nose about what someone else might do, but ultimately what others do cannot change who I am.

I had an unusual request from a friend of mine some time back: I was asked not to mention that I was a friend of hers. You see, I'm transgender. More than this, It's hardly a secret that I'm transgender—I am professionally transgender, as well as the founder of Trans Day of Remembrance. Her fear was that if someone knew that I knew her, then it would automatically be assumed that she was transgender, too.

It was a difficult thing to hear that my very existence was perceived as being enough to harm a person I called a friend. I try to harm no one in my daily affairs—yet here I was, being told that all I need to do to cause someone difficulty is to call them a friend.

I asked many of my friends who are transgender, in the wake of this incident, if they too would be uncomfortable being identified publicly as friends of mine. I consider these people close friends, I said, and still if this inadvertent outing would cause them trouble, I promised I would disclaim them immediately. Oddly, no one else seemed all that perturbed. I did not address this with my non-transgender friends, but maybe I should; presumably it will be a great shock to discover that merely being acquainted with me has the potential to cast doubt on their birth gender.

One of the first lessons I was taught at some of my earliest transgender support group meetings (more years ago than I usually would wish to admit) was that being in a group of transgender people exponentially raises the risk of being read as transgender. If you want to remain hidden, I was told, avoid others like you. Large group events would always require remote locations where we could all be hidden away; the concept of meeting with

27

your transgender siblings just anywhere was taboo. This was a world just a step away from secret handshakes and coded catch-phrases.

Much later, I learned that this divide-and-conquer strategy had been common in the older, university-based transsexuality programs of the 1970s. Associating with other transgender people could get you drummed out of the program. After all, you were supposed to be associating with those in your preferred gender, making strides down the road to Normal, not hanging about with others trying to take paths similar to yours.

While those gatekeeping systems are long gone, their survivors live on. Worse, these individuals, themselves transsexual, perpetuate the enforcement of the system they were required to navigate. If you don't fit the gender-norming rules they were expected to observe, you are a subject of derision, worthy of little more than the ridicule of your would-be peers. They have learned to construct a hierarchical order of who is acceptable and who is not.

Let me break it down this way: some lesbians and gays feel that their issues are more important than transgender issues, because transgender people are freaks. Some transgender people—often, but not only, transsexuals—view transsexual issues as more important than the issues of, say, cross-dressers. Some among the more genderqueer portions of our community look down upon those who opt to live in a more "normatively gendered" space. There are even groups that cross-dressers feel superior to: sissies, drag kings and queens, "little girls," and so on. Yes, I'm sure that we could follow even each of these groups and find that, eventually, everyone has someone they view as a freak.

This is a human phenomenon, and one which occurs especially, it seems, among marginalized groups. Trekkers versus trekkies versus people in Klingon costumes, or furries versus fursuiters versus, oh, plushies. I'm sure if I looked at model railroaders, I'd probably find that HO gauge fans look down at N scale, or something like that. The taxonomies are endless, often circular, and are usually graded to a fineness that would be invisible to any outsider. We just want to identify the "real" freaks, so we can feel closer to normal. In reality, not a single one of us is so magically normative as to claim the right to separate out the freaks from everyone else. We are all freaks to someone. Maybe even—if we're honest—to ourselves.

In the end, we find ourselves with one of two choices: do we push others like us away, to best fit in? Or do we seek out our kin, for comfort and company? For that matter, if we are all someone's "freak", does this mean we are all each other's "normal" too—and worthy of embrace?

These are questions I have asked myself, time and time again. I confess to having a phase during which I did not associate with other transgender people, for fear I would be guilty by association, or even get "tranny cooties." Maybe I was afraid I would see things in my own being I was not ready to face, or was afraid of challenging my own assumptions. I found it to be a very limiting way to live, and have chosen to embrace those I might see as my siblings.

Yes, even those who might be having a hard time embracing me.

This isn't to say that there's no such thing as defamation, or that everything is acceptable. Far from it. There is always a need to watch for attacks on us as a whole. We can't ignore right-wing demagogues who insist that the word of the doctor who proclaims a child's sex at birth somehow holds more sway over the reality of the body than the word of the person who inhabits it. Yet just as anyone can call me whatever they want, it is up to me to decide whether I care to answer. More than this, it should be irrelevant to me what any other transgender person opts to do. Their action does not somehow change who I am. It cannot.

I know what I am. I know that I've chosen to identify as a transgender woman, and that I am—by and large—happy with where I am in this world. I'm far from perfect, and I could give you a list as long as my arms of the things I'd love to change. Nevertheless, I am still here, and I am still me, and no one can change that without my permission.

At the same time, even though I am happy to identify as a transgender woman, I also applaud those who are seeking to redefine the notions of gender and are carving out spaces of their own. My own comfort is such that I'm glad to see other people out there challenging the assumptions and to know that their challenges do not necessarily pose a threat to my beliefs. Who knows—maybe my beliefs could stand a good challenge once in a while, and they might end up broader than they were before.

We live in a world of incredible variations, where there are some 200,000 species of moths and butterflies to be found in this planet, where one can find snowy ice caps and boiling cauldrons of lava, and where biodiversity is the very thing that keeps the whole complex system in tune. The notion of classifying things and then claiming that only this or that is a *proper* version of some being is a distinctly human construct, full of arrogance and hubris. When those of us who are gender outlaws of any stripe seek to set definitions on our realness, to determine who is somehow "normal" amongst us, it seems all the more crazy.

I assume it is some sort of human failing that makes us always need to shun someone who we perceive as "more different than thou." Some simply need to feel better about themselves by despising someone further down the chain from them. Nevertheless, this does not seem to help move us further along in the world at large.

We can worry about who is this and who is that, we can argue about who does or doesn't belong. We can talk about how much more legitimate one or another of us is. In the end, we are all somebody's freak—and basic human dignity is not a privilege of the lucky superior few, but a right of all or none.

Trans-Corporation: A benefit analysis of a transgender man in a corporate setting

CT Whitley

I'm hunkering down. My bunker is a tan particleboard desk enclosed by five-foot grey fabric partitions. I've become a corporate cadaver, entombed in my three-walled office illuminated in a fluorescent hue. A harsh voice bellows from the conference room. "You motherfuckers! You need to pull your heads out of your asses!" I take a deep breath. I've had my first lesson in high profile corporate interactions: learn to communicate so it isn't your ass getting chewed on the other side of that door.

This is not the touchy-feely environment I'd grown accustomed to during my liberal arts education in Sociology and Ethnic Studies. It's not an environment where I can capitalize on my queer theory and gender research by challenging the perception of gender norms in the work place. It's not a non-profit that holds diversity trainings or recognizes and values an array of differences. This is a company that records racial categories only to boost its EEO chart ratings, reducing the names on the chart to square boxes of Black, White, Asian, and Hispanic. Privilege is the sweat from management's pores, bonuses are the incentive, performance is everything, and cash reigns king.

During my two-year tenure as a financial officer in New York City, I grew increasingly aware of the gendered nuances of professional interactions in corporate culture, which reinforce binary systems, hamper communication between men and women, and frequently limit women's advancement. With this awareness, I moved at the periphery of categorized gender, shifting and shuffling through the expected communication patterns of my past and present genders. As a gender outlaw long accustomed to carving my own path, I learned to communicate in ways that were unavailable and unidentifiable to my non-transgender male and female coworkers, catapulting my own transgender status from corporate cost to corporate benefit. My female past and male present provided valuable reference points for negotiating interactions with both men and women. These days I rarely notice when I switch communication styles, sometimes even among different participants within a single conversation.

Just a few nights ago my partner asked, laughing, "You were talking to a man on the phone, weren't you?" I nodded, puzzled.

"How did you know?"

"When you talk to women, your voice is higher, you use more intonation, and you're more emotive," she said, "It's not that you become a woman, but you take on the communication style of one." She's right. In my journey, I have learned to call up elements of my past female life into my current male one when that style will strengthen my position. My masculine and feminine vocabularies meld to create negotiation platforms where I can understand and be understood without gendered limitations, expressing myself freely and clearly across sexes and genders.

While I understand sex and gender as socially constructed labels, I also understand that those labels are made real by their enforcement in dominant culture. Gendered behavior patterns were the key to at least half of miscommunication in my office. Therefore, this is not a deconstructive analysis, but rather a discussion of the realities of the gendered professional world. That world is built on the dominant culture's definitions of male, female, masculinity, femininity, and gay and straight, complete with the misogynist assumptions and biases the dominant culture bequeaths. While I neither believe in nor fit into these binary identity platforms, they nonetheless frame the corporate world. As a transgender man who has used my female past and male present to navigate an unknown world, I used my multi-gendered experience to challenge and manipulate the paradigm rather than to reinforce it; I was able to improve my office environment as well as to propel my career.

Thanks to my time in the queer spaces and liberal enclaves I've been a part of, I was able to view with fresh eyes the heteronormative world I worked in and its heavily gendered corporate interactions. In a corporate world where the infinite possibilities of sex, gender and sexuality went unnamed and unnoticed, gendered stereotypes about communication quickly proved useful. To be heard by men, brevity was key and intonation was a frivolous indulgence I could not afford, but cultivating the all-important air of dominance was well worth my while.

Part of my job was contract management; I would call directors and inform them of their ending contracts. When calling a man, I would say a quick hello and get to the point. "We have twenty-seven clients who need new contracts. I will bump up the value of the contracts, assuming you are okay with that?" They would answer a quick yes or no and I would return the phone to the receiver. By contrast, my female coworker would start with a friendly greeting, then scold him for not answering her emails or calling her back more quickly. After eight or nine minutes she would hang up the phone, excitedly reporting, "They said yes, yes, yes to everything I asked!" only to be livid later when nothing actually materialized.

Her conversation partner had stopped listening after the first "so how are the kids?" and hadn't heard any part of her real request. Lost in the material element of the call, the male colleague had missed the human element in the conversation, the point of real connection where community is developed. In this instance and others, my understanding of female and male communication styles allowed me to avoid the pitfalls of my more seasoned coworker, and my conscious study, awareness, and embodiment of male interactions facilitated my success with upper management.

In another instance, my department was tasked with a project that would have made Einstein sweat. In response to the stress, the non-transgender men hunkered down, stopped returning phone calls and focused solely on the task at hand, as though they were each an army of one. The women searched for reassurance from others, found community with other women by discussing their frustrations, made plans to go out at the end of the week, and leaned on social networks. These disparate responses, while effective for the individuals, created huge problems for the whole as neither side understood the other's stress-management techniques. I found that I could play the middleman, deftly switching roles so that in the presence of men I was isolated and hardworking and in the presence of women I was cooperative and sympathetic. The men stormed into my office grumbling, "She can't get anything done because she has to take time to talk to everyone. We have deadlines, can't she see that?"

Similarly, the women rushed in complaining, "He's so irritating, I try to talk to him to take the edge off and he shuts me down. He's so uncooperative!"

I listened sympathetically to each side's complaints, and then I worked my communication magic. With each side seeing me as an insider, I could venture a guess about what was going on across the gender divide, smoothing the tumultuous, gendered waters that threatened to flood the office with rage and dysfunction.

Interestingly, I was the first person in my position to receive high marks from both male and female coworkers. When I talked to male supervisors about past female employees in my position, they would say things like, "The men didn't find her to be effective. She made too many phone calls bothering directors about little stuff. The women liked her style, but I guess it's just because women tend to get along." When I asked about past male employees in my position, the same dynamic presented itself. Men found the male employee to be "more effective," but women found him to be "less connected." Both communication styles had something important to offer. Most importantly, because of the heteronormative patriarchy reinforced in those office spaces, it was often the communication styles of my female colleagues that were deemed frivolous, when in fact, their sense of community and collaboration reinforced cohesion, a sense of belonging, and unity among staff. Ironically, despite my openness about my transgender status, management didn't notice the bridge I was building over the gender divide. Nonetheless, I was getting promoted, even if my boss couldn't see that my success had one foot carefully balanced in the male world and the other in the female realm.

Despite the professional advancements women have made and continue to make since the 1960s, I think it is safe to say that many still hit a glass ceiling. My office was no exception. It is widely understood that "male" and "female" are constructed well before birth, which means that by the time a person enters the workforce he or she has had twenty to thirty years of standard gender construction and reinforcement woven into every fiber of the individual's life. This becomes a huge disadvantage for women. Women who are strong, determined, and free-willed are labeled 'lesbians' or 'bitches,' rejected for promotion because their deviation from socially accepted gender norms makes others uncomfortable. Women who present as feminine and communicate in a typically feminine manner see no upward mobility, regardless of their inputs into projects and discussions. Of course, outliers exist: women who can alter their performance of masculinity and femininity to interact with key people so that their outward performance is feminine, but their communication employs carefully selected "masculine" traits, like brevity and curtness. In my male-managed company, these women excelled.

Understanding socialized gender differences in communication is not merely about men expecting women to interact on their terms. It requires an ongoing discussion and assessment of office culture, politics, and engagement. It's not a one-day training on diversity, but a continual process of resocializing the self to use and understand various communication styles within and outside of a gendered context. Through this experience, I learned to value my journey as a transgender man by strategically utilizing my past and present to affect change and promote personal gain.

Over the past two years, I have challenged myself to articulate the communication differences in my office. I have experimented with changing my posture, tone, and style to address the men in management. I notice that in meetings where I was once invisible I am now addressed by management over my supervisor, a woman who has held her position for twenty-five years. It's a bittersweet moment, one where I realize I have mastered a new language. I am a bi-gender communicator. This is a point of joy in my life as a transgender male. I have crossed over to be heard as male by other men. However, power has infused me with a sense of responsibility as I have not always been in this position and can easily recognize the shift in power. In this recognition it is my responsibility to speak up when others are being silenced, to challenge the corporate communication style nested in a masculine paradigm. Knowing how to utilize and maximize communication styles between men and women helps me to be a better advocate, to assert my voice when others are being silenced.

In my years of transitioning, I often underestimated the complexity of my journey. I never imagined that I would be uniquely positioned to rise up the corporate ladder through my manipulation of gender. For those of us who have second-guessed ourselves, questioned our value, or been confronted with harassment and violence, I offer up this unlikely refuge: we can learn powerful life skills from our negotiation of gender divisions. Our differences are a powerful resource to reshape the social systems we are forced to engage in, even if we remain undercover.

Unfortunately, my corporate management not only perpetuated serious gender issues, but also fell victim to a severe lack of self-reflection, ultimately missing the invaluable perspectives of its employees. If they had recognized the bridge I represented between gendered communication styles, asked for advice, or simply acknowledged that my gender differences created a unique opportunity for them to learn, I could have been not just a behind-the-scenes asset, not just a self-promoter, but a visible, tangible proponent of the company's growth. My life's calling has since led me out of the corporate environment and into academia, but it is my hope that other gender outlaws working in corporations throughout the country will rise up out of their dimly lit cubicles to hold strategic conversations that directly challenge the cultural and political structures of their workplaces. Our voices, speaking from our breadth of experience, can transform dysfunctional companies into pinnacles of gendered bliss. Recognizing the heteronormative communication systems in the corporate world, we can challenge these dynamics from the inside. Becoming the medium of translation between the dual gendered system, we can begin to create spaces where those who have become silenced can speak.

A Slacker and Delinquent in Basketball Shoes

Raquel (Lucas) Platero Méndez

My decision to go *packing* tonight lends me a mix of optimism and poise that impels me to emphasize my masculinity, and with it, the prosthetic penis under my pants. I groom myself in front of the mirror. I make sure I have tamed my prebuilt curves. My hair looks carefully messed up and my new black shirt fits me surprisingly well. I think of how I look and I am unable to suppress a smile. I haven't made any plans, nor am I getting ready for a sexual encounter with someone I know. This is more a present to myself which makes me feel good every time I move; a small package that nonetheless changes my center of gravity.

I wonder, María Helena, if you would go *packing* tonight, if we would have a drink in some bar while we look at all the interesting girls, naughty half-smiles on our faces. All I know about you, María Helena N. G., is what a

1968 Francoist police record says. We don't know if you still live in Spain, if you still cross-dress to go out, or even if you are still alive, but your story affirms my reality across the decades that separate us.

A researcher, Victor Bedoya, found you in a bunch of yellowed papers discovered among a pile of records. You have a file number, a name, and all the venom of the oppressors who invoked article six of the 1954 *Ley de Vagos y Maleantes* upon you. This Law for Slackers and Delinquents is applied to homosexuals, pimps, and scoundrels; to professional beggars and to those who live from the mendicancy of others; and to those who exploit minors, the mentally disabled, or the handicapped, so that they undergo the following measures: a) They may be put in a work camp or farming colony. Homosexuals who are subjected to this security measure must be put in special institutions and must be, in all cases, completely separated from the rest of the criminals. b) They are not allowed to live in certain places or territories, and they have an obligation to register their address. c) They will be monitored by selected delegates.

The judge and the Civil Guard called you María Helena; they wanted to emphasize that you were a woman in their eyes. I will call you M. H.; it sounds more androgynous and up-to-date. M. H., if you could go out tonight with my buddies, still twenty-one years old the way you were that night in March of 1968, you might be the center of attention—though you would have to compete with other *dudes* such as my buddy Clark or myself. According to your arrest record, it pleased you to wear basketball sneakers and men's socks instead of the high-heeled shoes and pantyhose that were compulsory for women in those days. I believe you were ahead of your time. Your basketball sneakers are just like Clark's. You would probably have some other things in common with him beyond your shared hometown, Hospitalet, in Catalonia. Clark, or according to his I.D., Miriam, is going through bold and adventurous times. He is becoming aware of his desire to mold his body, to make it strong and muscular, adjusting it to the image he has of himself. What would you think of that, M. H.? Did you consider molding your body the way you liked it? Would you go to the gym with Clark? Would we talk about where to find men's clothes our size? We are *trannies*, you, Clark, and myself, and we would have a blast tonight, sharing a drink in our chosen space, mutual identities acknowledged.

Your appearance is meticulously described in your police record, as if they cared about nothing but what you were or weren't wearing. Forty years later, we don't usually identify socks and pants as transvestism, but clothes still mark gender norms. There are still social and psychiatric punishments when our masculinity exceeds acceptable limits, though we are not imprisoned for it in Spain. Even today, some men feel threatened by our "counterfeit" masculinity, and if someone is discovered "pretending" to be a man, the imposter is punished. In many ways, the world has changed, but not as much as we might like to think.

In your day, you went to *La Gran Cava*, a bar in Hospitalet, for a glass of wine. Tonight, Clark and I are going to do the same thing in Madrid. I can see you with your elbow on the bar, chatting noisily with the local cismen, and I try to imagine how the people from your hometown saw you. When Clark and I go out, they don't know if we are a couple of gay boys, two very masculine women, or just two freaks. When you didn't pass the *guy* test, M.H., the Civil Guard arrested you, taking you to the Atarazanas station on March 26th, 1968 to await trial before the Slackers and Delinquents judge.

In the eyes of the judge and the State, you, María Helena N. G., were a *woman cross-dressed as a man*, a socially dangerous person, engaged in the suspicious act of going out for a drink. Your mission was "to mislead women." It was unthinkable that women could freely want to be with you unless you lied to them.

In your time, women in Catalonia didn't go out to bars alone, nor did they enter spaces reserved for men. Being unaware of such social rules was not allowed. If you broke the norms it was presumed you had deliberately wanted to violate them. Therefore, you deserved not only social punishment from the State, but violence as well.

In your time, women existed only to perpetuate the social machinery of a weak fascist State: Forced to abandon the public sphere to which they had access during the Second Republic, they kept the family unit together as submissive mothers and wives (Pineda, 2008). The only alternatives to compulsory heterosexuality and motherhood were the convent, the lunatic asylum, or life as a selfless spinster. Anything else made you a socially dangerous person, a whore, a criminal. The psychiatry of the time regarded women as infantile, immature, and pathological, needing to be restrained by the civilizing influences of the National Catholicism Society, men, and the State (Vallejo and Martínez, 1939, pages 398-399 cfr. In Bandres and Llavona, 1996:8).

In your time, men were heads of their families, workers, and faithful patriots. Society exalted young and muscular bodies in fascist uniforms within the context of military comradeship (Pérez Sánchez, 2007). Yet the same men were feminized by their submissive position within the repressive system. Required to show virile attitudes, men had to perform masculinity in a precise and narrow way—segregated, almost to the point of homoeroticism—and were kept tightly under State, Church and Psychiatric control. Francoist eugenics aimed to foster a natalist heterosexuality while it reacted against moral degeneration brought by tourists and urbanism (Montferrer Tomas, 2003: 182).

You couldn't be a woman, because women didn't go out to have a glass of wine in a bar, nor did they relate to men as equals. You didn't have a family, a job, or a husband. Your boyfriend, himself a faggot, provided you an alibi, but that wouldn't help you tonight. The guards had you pegged for a transvestite.

Despite your "irresistible attraction toward women" and your "masculine tendency," you couldn't be a man. At the same time, these traits barred you from womanhood. You had exposed one of the main pillars of Francoism: the rigid order of gender and sexuality. You were born into a binary world full of good people and bad, saints and sinners, nationals and reds, men and women, heterosexuals and homosexuals. Heads of families and mothers were society's bulwarks against delinquents, socially dangerous people, and whores.

After the Civil War, the state, occupied with overcoming postwar miseries, delegated control of immoral behavior to the Catholic Church (Bastida Freijedo, 1986: 185). During the 1950s, moral and sexual panic spread and prompted the control of homosexuality. Primo de Rivera (1928) worked on a Napoleonic-style Penal Code that made homosexuality a "crime against honesty" and a public disgrace. Even though this Code was reformed during the Second Republic and the law against homosexuality was removed, the Law for Slackers and Delinquents was approved in 1933. Homosexuality was added to the list of dangers to society in 1954, during Francoism, which made being homosexual punishable with the full force of the law. The state was in charge of the imprisonment and control of "dangerous" individuals—homosexuals, pimps and scoundrels.

In 1970, the Ley de Peligrosidad y Rehabilitación Social (Law of Dangerousness and Social Rehabilitation, or LPRS) would add to this oppression by designing further measures of surveillance and control for "those people who carry out homosexual acts" (Pérez Canovas, 1996:20; Aliaga y Cortés, 1997: 29).

M. H., you lived during a regime that was especially concerned with transgressions that defied rules of morality and propriety. The judge who sentenced you, Antonio Sabater Tomás, genuinely worried about the dangers of such deviance, wrote extensively about *the infectiousness of homosexualism*. The authorities regarded you as a masculine woman and transvestite: an ugly woman and a defective man. They considered you a problematic heavy drinker who needed State intervention to control your instincts. It didn't help that you were a *beaner*, an ugly term for a Latin American immigrant. How telling that we use racist statements—gypsy, Moor, beaner—to speak of social, moral, and sexual degenerates (e.g. Sommerville, 2000:16 38).

M. H., if you, Clark, and I were to go out in Madrid today, our masculinity would be seen through social filters like class, race, ethnicity, and other lenses which normalize our appearance (Halberstam, 2007:198). Clark and I are white, middle-class, able-bodied urban professionals. All these factors influence how our masculinity—laden with the fissures of biologically female bodies—is read by every person we encounter. Despite our privilege, Clark and I often find our professional competence called into question because we do not look or act heteronormatively, because our gender and sexuality can be read ambiguously, and because we look working class and boyish.

M. H., even today you would still be a *beaner tranny*, unless you could adopt the right accent, skin color, and poise. Without a penny to your name, your masculinity would still be easily identified as working class. Visibly queer, you would still be grouped among the socially dangerous—sex workers, undocumented immigrants, HIV-positive people, scoundrels, and delinquents—potential allies forgotten by too many of today's sexual minorities.

These differences cut across the boundaries of time and space. The three of us are maladjusted figures, gender impostors who embody different versions of masculinity. We live in the space of non-definition; within binary parameters, we are not men but we aren't women either.

We mess up gender, sexuality, age, social class, race, social and professional competence, beauty, and mental sanity.

M. H., after your arrest they undressed you to examine your body and expose your curves ("the size of the clitoris is normal"), trying to determine what physiological traits and external influences might cause this kind of behavior in a biowoman. I shudder to imagine you naked before the eyes of Francoist oppressors. I think of all of us who have "deviant sexualities" and how we feel every time we go to the doctor; when we go through clinical protocols, legal procedures, or social practices which entail getting undressed or wearing rigidly-gendered clothes; when we have to develop a constructed male or female behavior, show the scars of our own choices and expose ourselves to other people's looks. I think about the different punishments we are exposed to; the way we are treated by our families, our bosses, and our co-workers; and the people we encounter socially. It makes me so angry that even today, some transgender people in Spain have had to strip naked and expose their bodies for permission to legally change their names.

M. H., I wonder if your parents supported you back then. Did they endorse the prevailing norms and reject your personal choices, or did they offer you support? Through the Hospitalet Civil Guard we know that your parents declared that they hadn't heard from you since you left their house on December 30, 1967. You made it only three months before you were arrested.

If you were a child of my time, would your parents have offered you more support in light of all the social changes that have taken place since? Did you need to leave in order to find your identity, to live outside the limits of your body and your biography? Our bodies betray us, allow others to judge us. Did they ask you, as many ask me: Why do you cut your hair like that? Why do you choose those kind of outfits when you could choose something nicer or more flattering?—always meaning something more feminine. How did you earn a living? Where did you live?

Maria Helena, for your crimes you were sentenced to a year and 127 days of internment; you were banned from Barcelona for two years and placed under surveillance for two additional years, as stipulated by the Law for Slackers and Delinquents. You were released on June 20, 1969, only two days after you were granted protective custody and transferred to the Alcázar de San Juan prison, when Judge Membrillera from the Barcelona Slackers and Delinquents court decreed "the dismissal of the revision of the measures imposed to the dangerous individual".

This story was recreated from a yellowed file in a forgotten box. Unfortunately, this police record is the only thing we know about you. María Helena N. G., you may still be alive, you may still have your pickups, still wear basketball shoes. I wish we could have met under those circumstances instead. Yet your story allows me to reveal the cost of making one's masculinity visible and to begin to understand the existence of visibly masculine women, transvestites, trans, you name it! In your day, I would have suffered a similar punishment. Getting to know you has made me feel accompanied, acknowledged, and, ironically, safe. Your past is a part of my past as well.

You made society acknowledge you, no matter the price. You stood as a transgressor who made the authorities feel questioned, so much so they had to punish you. Far from the current argument of invisibility when interpreting sexuality during Franco's dictatorship, your story shows that female bodies combined masculinity with an attraction towards women, and that both were read as a necessary threat that must be punished (Halberstam, 1998).

Your story invites us to ponder just how much the acceptance of gender ambiguity, masculine women, and trans people has changed in today's society. We still punish gender and sexuality transgressions; we still like to label people by sexual orientation, gender and sex. Many of us still have to wait until we are eighteen to have the right to our identities, many of us still have to prove that we don't suffer from a pathology, and many of us who profess non-dominant forms of masculinity and femininity still have to find spaces where we can belong. We are still socially controlled by our bodies and sexualities, and we still have to work extra hard to prove that we are as competent, beautiful, and healthy as everyone else.

Remembering, imagining, and recreating your story, M. H., is an act of resistance. To forget you would be typical of Fascist politics and culture, a colonialist *modus operandi* that dispossesses us of a possible imagery, of necessary referents that show us that our experience is always unique and unprecedented (Halberstam 2007). As we read your story, M. H., we are taking part in the creation of discontinuous and queer times and spaces which generate a locus of possibility to think about ourselves as livable and desirable bodies (Butler, 2006).

Today is Saturday and I am going to raise my glass of wine in a toast to you, M. H. To you and to all the trannies, faggots, and queers who reinvent ourselves every day.

The Old Folks at Home

Janet Hardy

Warm afternoon light, a small fireplace, hardwood floors clean in the middle and dusty in the corners. Shelves of books, dog toys scattered everywhere, plants on every surface, wind chimes trilling in the windows. Ikea furniture mixed with thrift-store finds and a couple of family heirlooms. Standard aging-liberal bungalow decor, really.

But: in the basement, several Hefty Bags, each marked with a strip of masking tape that says *drag*. In the converted garage on the first floor, a steamer trunk, dusty on top, full of S/M gear. On the main floor, my office, where I write the books that earn the money that pays for all this. On the top floor, our bedroom.

There are days when my spouse sits in the bedroom all day, coming down only to pee and eat. On those days, I try to find some work that I can bring upstairs, so I can sit next to him and we can touch occasionally. He watches TV with the captions on so as not to distract me, or plays games on his laptop, or dozes lightly, pain cutting channels from his nose to the corners of his mouth.

Last summer, in the front yard:

"I'd feel a lot better if I weren't so fat," I said, slapping my big thighs where they flattened out against the warm concrete step.

His back was to me; he was planting something. "Yeah...maybe if you got more exercise," he said. "And we should really be eating more fruits and vegetables." When he turned around to get another bulb out of the bag, I had my head in my hands and the sniffles were audible. "Oh, honey," he said, and sat down beside me on the step and put his arm around me. "What's wrong?"

"You weren't supposed to *agree* with me." My voice quivered.

"Ohhhhh..." he said, pondering. We sat together in the sun while I tried to get myself under control. He hugged me. "I'm so sorry, honey," he said, sincerely. "I keep thinking of you as a big dyke, and to a big dyke that wouldn't matter. But I forgot: you're a big fag, and *of course* it matters."

How could I not love a man like that?

I can't call him my "husband." I had one of those, and I know what the word means. It means someone who sighs and looks away when you overdraw the checking account. The person who made a beautiful garden so that I could enjoy it through my office window, who cooks enormous unclassifiable crock-pot concoctions that we can't finish in a week, who reminds me to drink enough water and to take my B vitamins so I won't get too stressed—that's my wife. When our close friends inquire after his health, they ask how my wife's been feeling lately. To everyone else, though, he's my spouse. It's an odd, stiff, unwieldy word, but it's the only one I've got.

Edward is six feet tall and thin. Enormous blue-gray eyes, long face, soft chin—sometimes he looks like David Bowie and sometimes like Bugs Bunny. His hair is a wavy wheatfield that would be the envy of many men half his age; he gets frustrated with its unruliness and wants to buzz it all off, and I beg him not to—I love to put my hands in it and feel its moist, coarse curls. Sometimes people tell us that we look alike, and I suppose I can see it—something perhaps in the large, slightly protruding eyes, or the teeth that make our dentist roll his eyes and sigh in distress.

He has perky little breasts. These days I don't think they look all that unusual; a lot of middle-aged men have breasts. But he tells me that when he was younger they got him glared at in the gay clubs—maybe because Edward likes his breasts, likes to wear tight T-shirts with the sleeves and neck cut away and the fabric worn thin so that his upper body looks like a teenaged girl's. I like this too; I've recently been pondering ways to instantaneously break in some more T-shirts to make them as soft, fine, and translucent as his old ones.

He has a beautiful voice, deep and precise and emotive as an old-time radio announcer; he says his high school drama teacher taught him to talk like that.

Some days he walks upright, at a pace not too much slower than mine. Most days, though, he leans heavily on a stout wooden cane, and I have to look back every few paces and stop while he catches up. Occasionally I'll see him from a distance—slow-gaited, forward-leaning, thick-spectacled, wearing a cap tipped over his eyes and several layers of sweatshirts and jackets—and mistake him for an old man. And then I go up to him and he grins, or sometimes grimaces, and the illusion is broken and I am relieved: not yet.

What's wrong with him? Nobody knows. We are now on our third expensive and temperamental neurologist. The injuries to his spine and joints, we know about: those happened twenty-five years ago, when he stepped between a baby stroller and a drunk driver. They account for the arthritis and maybe some of the muscle pain. But they don't account for the agony that comes on suddenly—every time in a different spot—and drops him to his knees, or the twinges in his hands and feet that he says feel like electricity shooting off the ends of his fingers and toes, or the poor coordination that means I must fill out the lengthy questionnaires that the neurologists demand and then ignore. Our family doctor, a good friend, says that for now we'll call it "Edward's Disease."

Edward's Disease means that I get to do most of the breadwinning, which is fine with me. My last partner let me earn all the money, too, and he didn't have anybody's disease.

Edward's Disease also means that we use the bedroom mostly for watching TV and cuddling and sleeping. That's less fine, but, you know, I'm fifty years old and I've had a lot more sex than most people. I go adventuring when I feel the need, and he's here waiting for me when I get back, and that's enough.

We got married late last year, at the Alameda County Courthouse. He wore a black suit I'd given him for Christmas. It fit perfectly and made him look sleek and urbane: definitely David Bowie. I saw him in it and immediately realized that what I'd planned to wear was frumpy and absurd. The bride is *supposed* to be the beautiful one, but I still ran out into the chaos of an after-Christmas sale and bought a new outfit to get married in.

The rings we exchanged are made of titanium, with a hammered finish. Of course, you can't hammer titanium. Some jeweler painstakingly made a mold with a hammered texture, and poured the molten titanium into it. But they look like hammered titanium rings. I love them: they're strong, and beautiful, and not exactly what they appear to be.

Most of our neighbors think we're a nice, ordinary, middle-aged couple. They don't know, or don't care, or are too polite to speculate about, what it might mean when a guy wears a tight T-shirt that shows off his breasts, or when a woman cuts her hair short and walks with a heavy-heeled swagger.

A few neighbors—the lesbian and gay man two doors down who got married and had a baby together, the mixed-race pair of aging sixties radicals across the street—know a different truth about us.

I'm not sure which picture is right, or if either one is.

I do know, though, that every night we turn out the lights, and I roll on my side and curl up, and softly, in the dark, the fronts of his long thin thighs press up against the backs of my short wide ones, and I feel my muscles soften and warm, and my eyelids grow heavy, and we are home.

Dear Austin Special Needs Bathroom

StormMiguel Florez

You. You understand. Always greeting me as soon as I get off the plane in Austin-Bergstrom International Airport. Always seeing me off. I think of you everywhere I go, wishing, longing for you. I find complete solace when I am with you. I have never felt safer than I do when I'm with you.

I just returned from Las Vegas and it made me realize how desperately I miss you. This long distance thing is killing me! I was in so many casinos and two airports and you weren't in any of them. When I looked for you in between the men's room and the women's room there was only a janitors' closet. I hated going into the women's room, but I had no choice. I felt so cheap. I hated the thought of you all the way in Austin while I went in there. It's just that it hurts me to wait for you. I mean literally. It physically hurts. I hope you understand why I had to do it. I am human. I have my needs. It meant nothing, I promise.

At one point I was in a restaurant in our hotel and I needed you so badly. I decided to make the long trek to my hotel room to relieve myself when my sister said she'd come with me. I told her I was going up to my room and she said, "There's a bathroom right outside the restaurant, just go in there." I explained that I hated public restrooms ('cept you of course, baby) and she said, "it's okay, you don't have to sit down on the seat." No one understands!

I remember the first time I saw you. I got off the plane in a strange new place feeling that itch I usually get when I travel, and there you were. I couldn't believe my eyes. I thought you were too good to be true. I remember approaching you cautiously, afraid of being rejected, but so intensely drawn to you that I couldn't stop. I had to know if you were for me. You opened your door, took me in, and I knew at last I had found what I've been looking for my whole entire life.

I've been with many others and have never felt quite right. In fact, it has always felt just plain wrong. It always does feel wrong, but I can't control myself long enough to see you. It would kill me, so I do what I have to do until I get to see you again. I can't wait until the next time. What is it, two more weeks? Then another month? It's torture.

I tell all my friends about you. They are impressed. I'd love for them all to get to meet you someday. You are my one true love. There is no other like you that I know of. Well, there was the bathroom at the Parkway Theater, but it's not the same. Not as good.

I'll see you soon.

Identity, Schmidentity

Telyn Kusalik

As a mixed-gender person, I am continually questioned about my gender identity. Sometimes people ask "How do you identify, gender-wise?" or "What pronouns do you use?" More often, it's simply the less sophisticated "Are you a woman or a man?" If I were a woman, or a man, these questions would be easy to answer. Since I'm neither of those two things, my answer is always long and complicated, and leads to an entire conversation about my identity. Instead of talking about bicycle repair, or how to make amazing vegan curry*, or the great German film that was screened last night, we end up talking about gender identity, and this is not what I prefer.

I move in the "radical queer" subculture, in which identity is a central concern. The main political paradigm in which we operate is identity politics: resisting the oppression of people of one identity group by people of another. People form communities based upon common identity, creating women-only spaces, trans-only spaces, people-of-color-only spaces. And, in my experience, people are at a loss for how to interact with me until they know how I identify.

For many reasons, I have concluded that identity is not central to my thinking. First, I am perfectly comfortable, in fact more comfortable, not choosing a fixed identity location; my own gender in particular is still mysterious to me. Secondly, I don't mind being referred to by terms that I don't identify with: I have no problem when people refer to me as a "transwoman," for example, despite the fact that I don't identify as one. Thirdly, I always feel uncomfortable in identity-based spaces, even spaces that make a particular effort to be inclusive of my identity. Unlike many of my peers, I don't think about myself or others primarily in terms of identity. Of course, like the culture that has shaped me, I often cannot avoid thinking about people in terms of identity. It comes more naturally to me, though, to think about people as united by their common *experience*.

For example: last summer, I experienced sexual harassment while buying a sandwich. The man behind the counter asked to see "what's under my skirt." As disgusted as I was with his behavior, I somehow felt obliged to stick around and let him finish making my sandwich rather than follow my instincts and run. I was feeling shaken after this experience, and the particular support I sought was from those friends who had endured similar harassment. In this instance, identity wasn't as important to me as experience.

To be sure, there is no denying that this experience of sexual harassment was a gendered experience. I am confident that if the man behind the counter had read me as a man, he wouldn't have said those things to me. And, certainly, the vast majority of my friends who had been sexually harassed were also read as women or girls when they were harassed.

It is important to note that the relevant factor to sexual harassment in this story is not gender *identity* but gender *perception*. Some friends and acquaintances who have experienced harassment do not, in fact, identify as women; they were *perceived* as women. As I sought support, the key issue was not their gender *identity*, but the gender *signifiers* that led them to be perceived as women. If we don't admit that sexual harassment is a *gendered* experience, we can never shed light on the sexism implicit in many cases of harassment. However, in addressing these sorts of gendered experiences, we may find that gender identity is not the most useful category.

It is this talk of gender as an abstract set of identity categories which I find unhelpful. I find no fascination in talking about how many genders there might be, or what the true meaning of "genderqueer" is, or what the difference is between third-gender and fourth-gender, or even which of my friends identify with which combinations of these gender words. I am uncomfortable when I am asked which gender I am or how I identify; I have little hope that telling people which of these abstract categories I identify with will help them know me better.

On the other hand, I am always happy to talk to people about my gendered experiences. For example, while the question "Are you a woman or a man?" is one I prefer not to answer, "How often are you perceived as a woman or a man?" is one that I love answering. Gender is a much more appealing topic of conversation for me when it is made concrete through experience.

I am uncomfortable in identity-based spaces such as women-only spaces and trans-only spaces, in part because I feel that identity categories are not necessarily the most relevant to the mission of the space. It seems to me that these "spaces" would be more effective if they organized themselves in terms of experience, rather than identity.

Consider, for example, a classic feminist space: a women-only gathering, dedicated to fighting sexism. The obvious (to me) reason for establishing a women-only mandate is that women are the ones who experience sexism, and thus have a special role in the fight against sexism. However, the organizers of such spaces forget that there are some men (I am thinking mainly of transmen here, but I'm sure that there are others too) who are often perceived as women, and thus experience sexism on a daily basis. There are also some women who are perceived as men and may experience sexism only rarely. While there are some forms of sexism that are felt by all (and only) those who identify as women, there are other forms that are felt by those who are *perceived* as women. Instead of creating space for those who identify as women, could we open our feminist space to all those who experience sexism? While this might create a space in which some members of the space experience sexism at the hands of other members of the space, this circumstance is just as likely to occur in a women-identified-only space.

For decades there has been a vocal part of the feminist community which attempts (and often succeeds) in keeping transwomen out of women's space on the grounds that they're not actually "real" women. For most of this time there has also been a very vocal group of transfolk and allies protesting this exclusion. Both sides rely on identity-based arguments to support their case. The question, as debated and discussed, is whether or not transwomen are women.

But the debate doesn't have to be about who *is* and *is not* a woman. These sorts of considerations become irrelevant if we start organizing our events, meetings, and working groups in terms of experience of sexism, rather than identity. I would venture that it is clear to all parties involved in the debate that most transwomen are perceived as women, and therefore experience sexism in many contexts. Even if a particular transwoman is being "read" as having an other than female history by someone policing gendered inclusion, she can point to her real-life experiences of sexism as evidence that she belongs.

One advantage of experience as a basis for a feminist space is that, if challenged, it is much easier to demonstrate how you are perceived than to prove that your identity is valid. This makes it more difficult for someone who is prejudiced against transwomen (or anyone else who they're not convinced is "really" a woman) to prevent them from accessing services or community.

Many contemporary feminists have recognized that there are many forms of sexism (like sexual objectification) that are experienced by transwomen, and other forms (like being unable to access an abortion) that are experienced by transmen. Thus these feminists have worked to create "women and trans" spaces that are open to both transmen and transwomen as well as ciswomen. This practice opens feminist space to some people who do not identify or perceive themselves as women, on the grounds that they experience sexism.

Regrettably, these "women and trans" spaces are still not open enough. There are people who experience sexism who would not necessarily identify as a woman or as trans. The ideal feminist space would be open to all those who experience sexism, whether that sexism is due to being perceived as a woman, due to having a uterus and/or ovaries and/or an estrogen-dominated hormonal balance, due to manifesting qualities that are seen as "feminine", or due to having a negative self-image caused by experiencing oneself as a woman in our sexist society.

Reorganizing feminist space to be inclusive of all those who experience sexism, regardless of their gender identity, would be only the first step. There are many other ways that we could work to create a culture which focuses on gendered experience rather than identity. We could talk about our sexual orientation in terms of what gender *presentations* we are attracted to rather than what *identities* we are attracted to. We could describe our friends and acquaintances to others using their experiences rather than using identity categories they belong to. I hope that we can move away from thinking about things in terms of identity and move towards a paradigm based upon experience.

*Telyn's Amazing Vegan Curry, Which Ey Would Much Rather Be Discussing

1/2 tsp cumin seeds
1/2 tsp mustard seeds
cooking oil
2 medium onions
4 medium carrots
1 large sweet potato or yam

curry spices to taste (depending what I have on hand, I use cumin, turmeric, and coriander, or prepared curry powder, or prepared curry paste)
1 can chickpeas
1/2 of a 14 oz. can of coconut milk

Place the cumin and mustard seeds in the bottom of a large pot, and cover in oil. Turn the burner on to medium, and chop the onions while the spices are being cooked out of the seeds. Throw the onions into the pot, and begin to sauté.

While the onions are cooking, peel and chop the sweet potato into quarter-inch cubes, and chop the carrots into pieces of about the same size. The onions should be well done by the time you have chopped the other vegetables. Add carrots and sweet potato, and cover. Stir every couple minutes; if the veggies start to stick, add half a cup of water. Let he veggies steam in their own juices for at least 15 minutes. Now is a good time to start rice or figure out any other side dishes.

Once the veggies are tender, add water to cover, and add chickpeas and seasonings. Bring almost to boiling and simmer for about 30 minutes, stirring regularly as this curry has a tendency to stick. Taste test to see if you need more spice (I always do). If there are still chunks of sweet potato and the curry is watery, simmer longer. It's ready when the sweet potato has turned to mush and thickened the liquid part of the curry. Turn off the heat, add coconut milk, stir, and serve with rice or naan bread and yogurt.

Letting My Light Out

Leona Lo

When the photobook *My Sisters, Their Stories* was published in 2003, I was thrust into the limelight as the first transsexual woman to lift the veil from the "invisible" transsexual community in Singapore. I was inundated with interview requests by local and international media. The more interviews I gave, the more confident I became in speaking up for transsexual rights, although I always said that I was speaking based on my personal experiences only. Over time I became known as a transgender "activist," but I always denied being one. I did not think I was qualified or brave enough to be an activist.

To be an activist of any sort in Singapore is to be an outlaw, but Singaporeans are not so sophisticated as to understand "outlaw"in its figurative sense. Thus, they described me as "radical." A "radical" is someone whose actions and ambitions depart from traditional social norms and expectations. In Singapore, normal means working in a nine to five job; getting married; buying a government flat—or, if you are more successful, a condominium by the coast and a country club membership.

Ironically, I hankered after some of these things too, but by virtue of having undergone sexual reassignment surgery—and not just that, but also outing myself—I was considered "radical." Being labelled "radical" in Singapore is not something to be proud of. It is equivalent to being slapped with a "toxic substances" label. Only in this way can my countrymen make sense of my role and place in Singapore.

An outlaw speaks and acts in socially transgressive ways. With the launch of my autobiography *From Leonard to Leona: A Singapore Transsexual's Journey to Womanhood*, my reputation as Singapore's transgender outlaw was sealed. Nonetheless, I still shied away from being seen as an "activist." I did not work actively and consistently to raise awareness of transgender issues; I addressed them only when a compelling opportunity arose, such as when I was ejected from a popular nightclub after being called a "ladyboy." Three events in 2009, however, would alter my perspective radically.

The first catalyst to my activism was an attempted takeover of a prominent Singapore women's rights group, AWARE (Association of Women for Action and Research). Over the years, AWARE had been quietly pushing the feminist agenda in Singapore. Along the way, the association created a small space for lesbian women to share their struggles, including the screening of a lesbian-themed movie and a Mother's Day event designed to be lesbian-friendly. In its sexual education curriculum for schools, AWARE positioned *homosexuality* as a neutral term, working to pave the way for a more accepting and tolerant learning environment for homosexual youth. Using this "gay agenda" as ammunition, a group of female parishioners from the notoriously right-wing fundamentalist Anglican parish, Church of our Saviour (COOS), staged a coup to oust AWARE's leadership at its annual general elections. Their actions came to national attention when a reporter from Singapore's flagship English daily *The Straits Times* broke the news. What ensued was a protracted battle (characterized in the media as a "catfight") which culminated in a dramatic showdown between the new and old guard and their supporters. For the first time, Singapore's lesbians and gay men emerged from the woodwork to back the previous leadership and orchestrate the ousting of the new guard. I not only blogged actively about the event, but was the only transgender woman participating in the climactic Extraordinary General Meeting (EGM).

With the AWARE incident, the Anglican Church revealed its fundamentalist agenda publicly for the first time, and was subsequently rebuffed by no less than Singapore's Prime Minister in his National Day Rally Speech. The coup leaders from the church were also booed off the stage at the EGM, paving the way for the old leadership to return. Unfortunately, this victory was short-lived. Bowing to public pressure, the Ministry of Education conducted a review of the Comprehensive Sexual Education program in schools and decided to drop AWARE as a sex education vendor until it "regained public trust" for its program. The Christian fundamentalists had triumphed in the classroom, blocking AWARE's small but significant effort to demolish negative stereotypes of homosexuality in the school setting.

I had encountered the Church Of Our Saviour before. More than a decade ago, when I was still a young pre-operative transsexual in transition, a leading ex-transsexual from COOS visited me, at my parents' invitation, to "counsel" me against going for surgery. He said he still harboured feelings for men, but did not express the feelings since they were sinful in the eyes of God. In retrospect, that was my first brush with the Christian fundamentalism of James Dobson's Focus on the Family, with which COOS is closely affiliated. With the AWARE incident, Singaporeans are only beginning to awaken to how deeply entrenched Christian fundamentalism is in our country and how its anti-gay and anti-trans agenda not only deforms the lives of LGBT youth, but also threatens national unity.

In August of the same year, I staged the *Ah Kua Show*, a one-woman play about my experiences growing up in Singapore. It was the celebration of a transgender voice that grows stronger with every assault—a voice of peaceful resistance framed in poetry and performance. I was touched when a group of students from my alma mater, Hwa Chong Junior College, came to watch the play and stayed behind to express words of admiration for my chosen path. For the first time, I felt vindicated and appreciated as a gender outlaw. The Anglican church may have triumphed in the classroom, but the new generation of Singapore students are not unthinking sheep. The truth—and the Internet revolution—has set them free.

Finally, in November 2009, the Anglican Archbishop, John Chew, spoke out against three "axes of evil" in Singapore: "homosexuality," "crass materialism," and, ironically, "religious fundamentalism." He attributed Singapore's breakdown in the family unit and decline in moral values to the alternative lifestyles of homosexuals, an extravagant claim indeed. This latest provocation by the Anglican church has strengthened my resolve to conduct research on the rise of Christian fundamentalism in Singapore, and to develop creative solutions to curb the excesses of the religious right. It is those of us who are already gender outlaws who must halt our society's progress down the slippery slope of discrimination and blame which has historically led ultimately to genocide.

> Ring the bells that still can ring;
> *Forget your perfect offering.*
> *There is a crack in everything*
> *That's how the light gets in.*
> —Leonard Cohen

Today, I, Leona Lo, no longer shy away from being known as a transgender activist. I aspire as well to the title "gay rights advocate." My knowledge and courage may not be perfect, but I believe that just by adding my voice to the peaceful chorus of resistance, I am already letting a little light in. Perhaps more than that, I am at last letting the light that is within me out into the world.

Impostor

Quince Mountain

I live a queer life, though I forget sometimes.

Last weekend, I sat with Mistress Magdalene and her slave, drinking chamomile. She calls me Q.

"Q," she asked, "do you know anyone who'd like to rent a room?"

I looked up from my tea, past the slave's shoulder. Though Magdalene's apartment is much homier than her dungeon, I had to consider what a prospective renter might think of the space. The mistress' living room is plush and penal all at once. Visitors are greeted with a pleasant table housing a bowl of fine, individually-wrapped chocolates and a fanned display of honest magazines like Vanity Fair. If the day has been rainy, they can place their umbrellas in the holder amidst a host of blue-eyed peacock feathers and assorted wooden canes. There's plenty of room to sit, even if one is leery of the suede dentist's chair. Oversized davenports upholstered with black faux fur line two sides of the room. On one of these is an overstuffed pillow where Roxy the Chihuahua lies resplendent in her diamond-studded collar. Sometimes I sit next to Roxy and wonder at the eyebolts on the wall. There are so many eyebolts. I can easily understand how Magdalene earned a preferred business account at Home Depot, which she calls Dom Depot.

"Great place in a pinch—" she says, "it's open long after the others have closed." Though I am curious exactly which requests have constituted "a pinch" for Maggie over the years, I've never asked. I figure she gets enough questions about work from her mother.

"Uh, sorry," I mutter, "I don't know anyone who's looking for a room right now—no one who'd fit."

The truth is, I know plenty of people who might fit. So many of my friends are nocturnal, living off the grid, decidedly outside Reproductive Standard Time. They are knowing and ambitious, sharp-taloned and exquisitely plumed. My life is full of cowbois and midwives, straw bale homeowners, go-go boys, gutterpunx, hobos, herbalists, and enough poets to fill a homeless shelter. Some of these folks are remarkably humble, but there are packs of proud people, too. There are proud Deaf people and proud gay people, proud round people and proud country people. Pride in such earthy colors and shapes: a virtual cornucopia of the deadliest sin.

What is it, then, that keeps me from referring anyone to the roommate-seeking Mistress? Is it the shape of my own pride? Why this reluctance to help a friend? Do I not think she'd make a good landlord?

I think it's this: against the backdrop of my colorful, queer world, I look pretty damn straight. Sitting under this menacing arch of metal rings, I feel as I imagine most any reasonably open-minded straight guy might: warmed by the welcome of friends, awed by the strange elegance of this home-cum-dungeonette, impressed at the life choices of another (so different from my own) and, I'll admit, fairly dissatisfied with the strength to which the slave has brewed the tea. I feel so normal, definitely not colorful enough for my friends. Magdalene throws me a bone, but how am I qualified to be her housemate referral service? I'm a little awkward, yes. And in Junior High School I was harassed more than the average tomboy. But that was so long ago; now I'm just another guy with a nine-to-five. I'm not out there on the edge. I'm not shaping our community. I'm a relatively law-abiding citizen, an aspiring writer: a B-list queer. Maggie invites me over because I like her poems, maybe because I bring venison jerky, but certainly not on my own merit. I've somehow managed to foist my way into a community to which I don't really belong. It's great to feel a part of things, to hear the latest news from the queer underground. But one day soon, my friends will figure out that their faith in my suitability was unwarranted, that I'm not nearly as deliberate as they are: not as savvy, not as creative, not as committed to the movement, any movement. I want health insurance; I say 'no' to drugs; I read the Times. I come in a funny package, maybe, but I'm just another sad-sack citizen, another namby-pamb purveyor of the pervasive paradigm. My friends are the seeds of resistance, and I am the chaff.

Knowing that secret, the no doubt soon-to-be-unearthed secret of my imposture, how could I in good faith hook up the Mistress with a new roomie? Two years from now, when my friend (let's say it's Porkchop, the straw bale homeowner whose first straw bale home isn't faring as well as planned) and Maggie invite me over for Solstice, I'll know in my sad suburban heart that the invitation was made out of obligation, that, having had time to compare notes, my friends will have discovered I'm a poseur. They will still be inclined to recognize me as instrumental in their union. But, once exposed, what value will I retain? My friends are so much worthier. And I'm just not ready to face myself, to face that kind of dismissal. So I say, "Nope, can't think of anyone in the market," and a few minutes later I suck down the dregs of my drink and excuse myself.

Out on the street as I walk to my truck, a flickering porch lamp highlights my solitude. I want a porch one day, a home: yet another vanilla inclination. And just as I'm working up a really sweet daydream about my very own asphalt driveway, a dude emerges underneath the lamp. Walking right at me, he says, "Freak." He brushes past me. "What the fuck are you?" he asks, expecting no answer.

None of us, in a vacuum, is queer. We are each only a small thing. What I realize, though, in the aftermath of Mr. What-the-fuck-are-you?, is that the small thing I am is somehow enough to identify me as part of an enormous, queer thing, something that can never be about a single person. The dude on the street didn't really want to know what I am. He asked precisely because he thought he knew, and, in doing so, he reminded me of the community to which I indeed belong. No, I am not colorful enough, not queer enough to reshape the world. It turns out, no one of us is.

I pull out my phone, suddenly brave and wanting to hit Magdalene about the roommate sitch. "Actually, I know someone who'd be really great," I begin when she answers; "His house is falling down."

Jihad

Azadeh Arsanjani

jihad

my running-girl heart

queer

is exhausted

jihad

from dragging around

queer

all the wrong definitions

jihad

of these blood words

queer

that white people

jihad

won't stop saying

queer

and when they say them, meaning me.

jihad

I am a brown girl in struggle,

queer

like every brown girl in struggle,

jihad

and if some of us have not been girls for very long,

queer

we make up for it in struggle.

jihad

okhty, please trust

queer

that on the glorious day when I come home

jihad

my bags will be full of meat and fruits

queer

we hunger together, and we will feast together.

Are You a Boy or a Girl?

Roe-Anne Alexander

interlude

But the real watershed moment? The instant in time in which I knew that I HAD to change, to give up whatever had to be given up, to create myself in my own image, to transition? An early-evening showing of *Friday Night Lights*.

Yes, the football movie.

After high school, I had watched *Lucas* 9,000 times, reveling sadly in Corey Haim's football misfit. Years later, confronted with *Friday Night Lights,* I suddenly could no longer pretend. I was so angry that I had been denied football—the sport for which my dad had, for whatever reason, tried to groom me—and I was so sad. They talk about people's lives flashing before their eyes when they die—the life I should have had flashed before my eyes after the movie. Me, being hazed, but not beaten, by the football team. Me, in my varsity letter jacket. Me, playing small safety (or, joy of joys, wide receiver!) in college, probably Colorado or Georgia or maybe someplace in California. Me, writing stories after college, getting published, teaching. Me, a boy, lanky like my brother, narrow-hipped, no-breasted.

Me, in other words, as myself.

—Rafe Posey

Being reconfigured is not the same as being reimagined.

Part Two

The Big Reveal

Sherilyn Connelly

A scene from a 1984 35mm straight porn movie called *L'Amour* goes like this: in a neon-drenched bar which gives the film immediate value as a historical piece, straight male porn legend Harry Reems asks straight male porn demigod Jamie Gillis why women can't be more like men. It really makes no sense except to telegraph the inevitable punchline. A couple of girls identified in the credits as Ivory Essex and Rachel Whitney throw themselves at the boys (duh, it's porn) and fellatio follows.

Jamie and Rachel fuck as Ivory continues to blow Harry. After a money shot in which Jamie ruins Rachel's perfectly nice black gloves, Ivory stands in front of Harry, lifts her skirt to reveal a Dirk Diggler-esque penis, and says: "And now, boys, we're going to have some real fun." Harry says: "Oh, no we aren't!" He and Jamie then rush out of the room, their pants literally around their ankles but their heteromasculinity intact. Ivory laughs and calls them chicken as they run away. Power, sister! Joke 'em if they can't take a fuck!

I encountered the clip on a shemale porn compilation tape from the mid-nineties with the painfully unimaginative name *The Best of Both Worlds*. The scene felt like the historical artifact that it was; the rest of the tape was more recent, plotless shot-on-video scenes in which the shemale got to do more than just suck off the man, and the man didn't run away in the grip of homosexual panic.

In most modern "reveal" scenes, the guy uses every acting skill he has in an attempt to appear surprised. He usually looks like he's found a bug in his food, calls it extra protein, and keeps eating. The scene in *L'Amour* was significantly different in that it showed the fear generated by "chicks with dicks." I suspect it represented the way most straight bio-men felt, and still feel.

I have never seen a porn movie in which the transsexual is hurt or killed as a result of her secret being revealed. It has happened on more than one occasion in "respectable" mainstream movies, such as *The Crying Game*, in which the much-hyped reveal scene is followed by the ostensible hero giving the girl a bloody nose, then retching for a minute straight. All things considered, I'll take being fetishized as a sex object over being assaulted or killed as an unnatural freak.

As may be obvious by now, shemale porn is my favorite kind. The reason is simple: representation. In it, I can actually see people who look like me. My heart and soul are female, but it's not how I was born; I look more like shemale porn star Joanna Jet than genetic female porn star Jenna Jameson. I think Joanna's prettier anyway.

Growing up, empirical evidence suggested I was a boy. Everyone told me I was a boy; I was the youngest of four boys; I had three brothers who were boys *just like me* except older. Not that it was drilled into my head *per se*; it was just how things were, and I didn't have any sisters around for comparison.

I knew early on that the "boy" thing wasn't really right for me, but I didn't have the language to express it, and movies and television taught me that boys who wanted to be girls were not received very well. In any event, my penis never really entered into the equation. Its primary *raison d'être* was piddling and the occasional ill-timed boner, usually when I had to stand up in class. Otherwise, it was just kinda there.

Melodramatic reveal scenes notwithstanding, what shemale porn taught me as a deeply closeted teenager was that a girl with a dick could be just as sexy and hot as genetic girls. (It's sensationalized, but, duh, it's porn.) I looked like a gawky, schlumpy boy, and I didn't find the temerity to transition until my mid-twenties, but shemale porn stars were always among my heroes.

The typical scene went like this: the guy and transsexual flirt, maybe kiss some. Even though she was kissing a boy, that was often the hottest part for me, the simple face to face intimacy. She then sucks his dick, and he might fondle her breasts. (Horribly fake breasts, but duh, it's porn. At least the transsexuals have an excuse to have obviously fake breasts.) Her panties are pulled down, revealing her dick. He then fucks her in the ass, pulls out, and jorm issues from his penis onto her face and/or body. The end.

Very rarely would the boy suck her dick, and even rarer still would the boy get fucked by the transsexual, using either a toy or her own biological equipment. More often, her dick is unused, pendulumming back and forth as he rams her, neither involved in the action nor commented upon. The boy never even has the goddamn courtesy to give her a reacharound.

The holy grail for me was girl-and-transsexual scenes. They existed sporadically at best, since the primary market was men. Though they probably liked the lesbianic nature of such scenes, those men wanted to see themselves represented just as much as I wanted to see myself, and they were shelling out considerably more money. As a result, I had to fast-forward through a *lot* of mediocre-to-dreadful stuff to get to those few really good parts, but, duh, it's porn. Of course, that's the ratio with mainstream media as well.

Then and now, I like scenes of a transsexual with a pretty genetic girl. A pretty transsexual with a genetic girl is even better. But a pretty transsexual with a pretty genetic girl is one of the sexiest things ever to me, since I aspire to be a pretty transsexual and I'm attracted to pretty genetic girls. Often the girl is Sharon Kane, who looks like Courtney Love's older sister. For me, that increases the hotness by a factor of ten. Your mileage may vary.

One "reveal" scene in particular had quite an impact on me. She was a tranny of Latin American extraction, beautiful body, long black hair, just hot all around. Her dick, however, was shriveled like a deflated balloon.

This was rather unusual. Like most any other kind of porn involving biological males, the emphasis in tranny porn is the penis, even if only the boy's gets any play. (If there are no biological males involved, the dick is made of rubber or silicone.) But most of the audience wants to see a pretty tranny with a large or least healthy-looking member. There's a reason why the career of a tranny porn star grinds to a halt if she gets vaginoplasty, aka sexual reassignment surgery: she ceases to be a chick with a dick and is now just a chick. That market is quite saturated, and the beauty standards are different.

Watching this scene as a teenager, I saw how I wanted my body to look, and I knew that it would require hormones. They already held a sort of magic-pill reputation based on what little I'd read, but now I was convinced she was a prime example of the hormonal feminization process. It seemed logical: the smaller and more atrophied the penis because of hormones, the more female the face and body. Hell yeah! Sign me up for *that!*

These days, I realize that she had the advantage of starting hormones at an early age, and most likely had been castrated around the same time as well, making the impact of the estrogen that much stronger. In polite Western culture, castration tends to be referred to as "orchidectomy," which means the removal of the orchids, i.e. the testes. It's used for the same reason as any euphemism: the protection of delicate sensibilities. Sometimes I think that if there's ever going to be world peace, humanity will have to get over its collective castration anxiety. Which means there's never going to be world peace, but we knew that already.

Anyway, there was no such luck for me on either the hormone or castration count, and certainly not as a teenager. I also realize that my usage of the words "luck" and "advantage" are questionable, as there's a very real possibility she was feminized nonconsensually and sold into sexual slavery. Even now, as a progressive sex-positive queer San Francisco hipster who recognizes the severe ethical issues involved, it's difficult not to be a little envious of those who were automatically granted what I couldn't bring myself to ask for.

I mean, I can only imagine the fireworks if I had taken the tape to my Mom and said: "Here! This! Want! Me! Can I? Please?" Even using complete sentences wouldn't have helped. I could barely admit the desire to myself, and the closest I could come to hinting at it was telling my girlfriend that I was interested in crossdressing—which, in retrospect, was pretty brave for a seventeen year-old in 1991 Fresno.

I did finally start on hormones and a testosterone blocker at the ripe old age of twenty-five. As I write this, I'm on the eve of my thirty-fourth birthday. I have not been physically castrated (mainly because I keep forgetting to actually make an appointment), and there's no atrophy or shrinking to report.

Not that I'm sure I would notice. Another revelation brought to me as a teenager courtesy of porn was the fact that dicks, on trannies or otherwise, are generally much larger than mine. Statistically speaking, my penis when erect is still smaller than the average flaccid penis. It's more like an overachieving clitoris with a urethra than what's considered a schlong in this society. Or a cock. Even "prick" gives it too much credit. A weenie, perhaps, or half a Vienna sausage.

Which is fine by me. On a purely practical level it means bulge isn't an issue unless I wear tight clothes like bike shorts, and I don't need to tuck, the method wherein the penis is hidden back between the asscheeks. Mine doesn't even reach the chode. For that matter, when a girlfriend once explained the concept of riding to the left or right—that is, which trouser leg the snake hides in—it was alien to me. It had simply never been an issue, because instead of needing to go to the right or left, my penis stays right there in the middle, more often than not shrunk back into the scrotum like a frightened turtle.

In the guilt-by-biological-association department, there's the "male energy" issue—that is to say, because I have a penis, I exude male energy and thus am a threat to certain Mission District bathhouses and Midwestern music festivals. Yeah, right. To call my penis a source of male energy is like saying an expired watch battery is a source of electrical energy for San Francisco, since my penis and the battery generate roughly equivalent power. And in a city whose chief exports are artificial testosterone and anatomically correct dishwasher-safe strap-on dildos, the "penis equals potential rapist" argument is so fracking absurd and reductionist and downright hypocritical that I'm not even going to address it here. Beyond the previous sentence, I mean.

All of which accounts for why my personal gender identity has never really been affected one way or the other by my penis. It's just so small and unobtrusive, lacking sound and fury yet not signifying a damn thing. What's more, I totally missed out on the "dick equals privilege" socialization. I don't know how it worked with other biological males, especially ones raised with older brothers and no sisters, but nobody bothered to tell me that having a dick made me a first-class citizen. It wasn't until I was a teenager that it really struck me how phallus-worshipping human society is, and by that point, I didn't care. Whatever. Mine didn't show, and it was nobody else's concern unless I got intimate with them, and even then it would be okay, yes?

As it turned out . . . yes. My own personal reveal scenes have been drama-free. No lover has ever reacted negatively about my penis, either regarding its size or its very existence, before or after transition. It's simply how I am, and anyone who's inclined to have sex with me in the first place has probably already accepted that I may be so equipped.

Some of us don't like to take the chance, or can't get past what the organ represents. One of the first trannies I met, back in the mid-nineties before I started transitioning, would have sooner eaten a bullet than let anyone near her mysterious genitals. She wore a thick latexy contraption which smoothed her crotch of any possible personality, and wouldn't even take it off during our few fumbling attempts at sex. As far as she was concerned her dick was the root of all her problems, and eventual vagino-plasty was the cure.

Me, not so much. I'm not opposed to the idea, but I'd also like to get a tummy tuck and see the Aurora Borealis and try a vac-bed and have Joan Didion give my first novel a glowing writeup in the *The New York Review of Books*. Maybe I'll someday have the time and resources, but putting vagino-plasty at the top of my personal Must-Have list would be a path to madness.

Besides, my anecdotal understanding of the process is that the larger the penis, the deeper the vagina, and the greater the overall chance of the surgery being successful, since there's more raw material to work with. Ivory probably has a great one by now. I'm rather lacking raw material, so maybe it's not meant to be, and that's okay. I'm not a boy because I have a penis, and just because I don't have a vagina doesn't mean I'm not a girl.

The Wrong Body

Scott Turner Schofield

Doctors wonder, want to know exactly what makes a person transgender. They hypothesize a rush of hormones at the wrong time, brought on by stress perhaps? They want to find a simple reason, a diagnosis, a cure to make life easier.

I believe it is sheer will.

Yes, embryonic me imagined life infinitely more interesting as a trade between soul and body. And so, here I am. I was not born in the wrong body.

My father fooled around with a nineteen-year-old woman at a crucial moment in my fetal development. My mother caught them in the middle of it, wrapped around one another like baby twins. Call it a rush of blood to her head: I bathed in the trickledown of emotions when she kicked him out.

After their breakup, my father broke into the family storage space filled with the treasures he and my mother had saved for their new life as parents, for the time when they could afford to move out of their trailer and into a house together. My mother had taken their money for me, and so he took an ax to all of their things, smashing furniture, slashing sun dresses, shredding photographs: cutting their shared possessions in half.

Imagine embryo me, inside my mother, walking into that chaos.

Can you feel the hurricane flood of betrayal over love, hot anger and deep sadness rushing in torrents of estrogen, testosterone, and progesterone over baby me, cleaving gender from sex, body from self.

There was no room for another man in my mother's life, only me. Swimming as best I could in this cascade of confusion, I chose to delight my mother by being born a baby girl. I knew even then that she, too, would attempt the impossible for me.

As lines creased into my fetal hands, I chose to be born a baby girl because I saw that I would have time to appreciate my journey, with the head to understand it as a gift and the heart to achieve my whole self through all of the trials it takes. Curled in her warmth, nourished by her food, protected by her very skin, I could feel my mother's desire for my best life. Back then, she held me so that I could be certain that I would have the love and support to find my way later.

Furthermore, I knew that being born female would build a bridge to the kind of man I wanted to become: a man unlike that father in every way. Being born female makes me a man that good men may look to for ways to understand and honor women, a person that people may look to for ways to find and appreciate themselves. Like they say, "mistakes" are just lessons waiting to be learned.

Trauma or no, I would have been trans no matter what body I'd been born with. Tell the doctors that we exist for the health of humanity, which needs to find wholeness and belief in complexity. Girl in boy's body or boy inside a girl; call it fate or biology, will, or spiritual choice. But I was not born in the wrong body.

Performance Piece

Julia Serano

If one more person tells me that "all gender is performance," I think I am going to strangle them. Perhaps most annoying about that sound-bite is the somewhat snooty "I-took-a-gender-studies-class-and-you-didn't" sort of way in which it is most often recited, a magnificent irony given the way that phrase dumbs down gender. It is a crass oversimplification, as ridiculous as saying all gender is genitals, all gender is chromosomes, or all gender is socialization. In reality, gender is all of these things and more. In fact, if there's one thing that all of us should be able to agree on, it's that gender is a confusing and complicated mess. It's like a junior high school mixer, where our bodies and our internal desires awkwardly dance with one another, and with all the external expectations that other people place on us.

Sure, I can perform gender: I can curtsy, or throw like a girl, or bat my eyelashes. But *performance* doesn't explain why certain behaviors and ways of being come to me more naturally than others. It offers no insight into the countless restless nights I spent as a pre-teen wrestling with the inexplicable feeling that I should be female. It doesn't capture the very real physical and emotional changes that I experienced when I hormonally transitioned from testosterone to estrogen. *Performance* doesn't even begin to address the fact that, during my transition, I acted the same, wore the same T-shirts, jeans, and sneakers that I always had, yet once other people started reading me as female, they began treating me very differently. When we talk about my gender as though it were a performance, we let the audience—with all their expectations, prejudices, and presumptions—completely off the hook.

Look, I know that many contemporary queer folks and feminists embrace mantras like "all gender is performance," "all gender is drag," and "gender is just a construct." They seem empowered by the way these sayings give the impression that gender is merely a fiction. A facade. A figment of our imaginations, endlessly mutable and malleable. And of course, this is a convenient strategy, provided that you're not a trans woman who lacks the means to change her legal sex to female, and who thus runs the very real risk of being locked up in an all-male jail cell. Provided that you're not a trans man who has to navigate the discrepancy between his male identity and female history during job interviews and first dates. Whenever I hear someone who has not had a transsexual experience say that gender is just a construct or merely a performance, it always reminds me of that Stephen Colbert gag where he insists that he doesn't see race.* It's easy to fictionalize an issue when you're not aware of the many ways in which you are privileged by it.

Almost every day of my life I deal with people who insist on seeing my femaleness as fake. People who make a point of calling me effeminate rather than feminine. People who slip up my pronouns, but only after they find out that I'm trans, never beforehand. People who insist on third-sexing me with labels like MTF, boy-girl, he-she, she-male, ze & hir—anything but simply female. Because I'm transsexual, I am sometimes accused of impersonation or deception when I am simply being myself. So it seems to me that this strategy of fictionalizing gender will only ever serve to marginalize me further.

So I ask you: Can't we find new ways of speaking? Shouldn't we be championing new slogans that empower all of us, whether trans or non-trans, queer or straight, female and/or male and/or none of the above?

Instead of saying that all gender is this or all gender is that, let's recognize that the word gender has scores of meanings built into it. It's an amalgamation of bodies, identities, and life experiences, subconscious urges, sensations, and behaviors, some of which develop organically, and others which are shaped by language and culture. Instead of saying that gender is any one single thing, let's start describing it as a holistic experience.

Instead of saying that all gender is performance, let's admit that sometimes gender is an act, and other times it isn't. And since we can't get inside one another's minds, we have no way of knowing whether any given person's gender is sincere or contrived. Let's fess up to the fact that when we make judgments about other people's genders, we're typically basing it on our own assumptions (and we all know what happens when you assume, right?).

Let's stop claiming that certain genders and sexualities "reinforce the gender binary." In the past, that tactic has been used to dismiss butches and femmes, bisexuals, trans folks and our partners, and feminine people of every persuasion. Gender isn't simply some faucet that we can turn on and off in order to appease other people, whether they be heterosexist bigots or queerer-than-thou hipsters. How about this: Let's stop pretending that we have all the answers, because when it comes to gender, none of us is fucking omniscient.

Instead of trying to fictionalize gender, let's talk about the moments in life when gender feels all too real. Because gender doesn't feel like drag when you're a young trans child begging your parents not to cut your hair or not to force you to wear that dress. And gender doesn't feel like a performance when, for the first time in your life, you feel safe and empowered enough to express yourself in ways that resonate with you, rather than remaining closeted for the benefit of others. And gender doesn't feel like a construct when you finally find that special person whose body, personality, identity, and energy feels like a perfect fit with yours. Let's stop trying to deconstruct gender into nonexistence, and instead start celebrating it as inexplicable, varied, profound, and intricate.

So don't you dare dismiss my gender as construct, drag, or performance. My gender is a work of non-fiction.

---

*In his television show "The Colbert Report," Stephen Colbert plays a fictional right-wing political pundit. Satirizing conservatives who insist that racism no longer exists in America or that we are now living in a "post-race" world, Stephen's character regularly claims that he doesn't see race, and that "People tell me I'm white, and I believe them...."

The Perfect Storm

Sam Peterson

I think it may be time to embrace the next wave of feminism. When I suggest this, my partner muses, "Do we actually need another wave? Or have we evolved past that?"

We need another wave. Feminism has absorbed most of its tail and is hopping towards a verdant central isle, but we're still just frogs, really, aren't we?

Fourth Wave feminism is distinctly trans. I think when we no longer need gender identification at all we can thank the waves that washed us and our tender, rubbery limbs ashore, but until that time, let's surf this together, shall we?

The Fourth Wave is not generational. I was born in 1960, and was steeped in the womyn-cast cauldron of Second Wave witchery. My first science-fair exhibition was a planet being explored by "all-women astronauts." (In space, no one can feel the glass ceiling!) absorbed the lessons of those important decades, and then sat at the feet of my younger knitting sisters of the Third Wave, gleaning wisdom from them as we needle-pointed Nico on a pillowcase while bending our boyfriends over.

The Fourth Wave urges intolerance appraisals. I am constantly mortified by what old, bad ideas have managed to creep back into my cupboard, or worse. Prejudices get in like sugar ants in the kitchen: They find a miniscule leaving from a disgusted fruit and there's a swarm. All of a sudden it seems okay for me to talk smack about fat people, or fags, and the next thing I know I'm having to Hazmat the entire storeroom. These self-scrutinies are the regular checkup, the testicle I knead for marbles and peas, and I can do it myself now that I have the how-to manual crafted from the frontlines of the Third. Intersectionality is the paperweight holding down the pile of systems of oppression, a clear acrylic pyramid with labels floating like unhappy confetti: poor, African-American, queer, disabled, blue-collar. The Fourth Wave has no classification, no bureaucracy, and it likes to touch itself.

While the Fourth Wave resists being named at all, it knows, as all transpeople know in our marrow, the meaning of fixity. Fixed ideas, fixed genders—stasis at all—is a little death, and not in that fun, French petit mort way. Fixity is what made my bones leaden and who stuffed my body into starchy slips and knee socks when these knees were made for corduroy and band-aids. This new feminism is compassion: ever softening, ever bending to meet you, ever stroking the cheek of the outcast fairy princess boys. It is Neverland for the bullied and broken who can finally be children—not forever, but at last.

Most humans evade change, spend a lifetime avoiding death. Transpeople do not have this ersatz luxury. Our change is neither seasonal nor cyclical; it is a literal embodiment of the atomic dance. Our chemistries jig while we watch ourselves die and transform, and if we are on hormones our dendrites race into this new neurochemical sea, leaving the foamy remnants of a former person in their wake.

Fourth Wave is not about the Third Sex; it's about the Third Eye. Lest we forget, transpeople are made entirely of light, and we are here to blast forth from our collective skulls, smiting all the shibboleths, seducing the sacred cows with particles of divine love. The party's tired, so it's time to bring the Glow Sticks. Even we codgers can move to the next phase, the dance floor where boi and grrl merge in a beautiful disco kaleidoscope, becoming something whose meaning resists translation, is so inscrutable it defies category, but whose moves, whether spastic or elastic, generate the warmest rays of light. Activists need to be Sagittarian by nature, always looking to hoof it, ready to trot to the next, better place. The dance hall beckons.

Third Wave feminism expanded the landscape, embraced kink, scraped off the mold of dogma, and explained how someone could dress like a little girl in public, be a Daddy in bed, and still be a feminist. As the Third Wave adopted Bettie Page, Fourth Wave looks at the Daddy/little girl construct with hot nostalgia. We don't discard: We use everything, because we're green like that. I'll bust out my Daddy when appropriate, but my sexual gender is a mutant cephalopod with more limbs than Kali-ma, and they all want to embrace and caress and beat you into a delicate froth of submission.

Transpeople are either mutants or the next evolutionary stage: Either way, it looks like it's gonna be great TV. We best pay attention now and not TiVo for later. Trans is here to blow the lid off: off the Tupperware container of marriage of any flavor, off the top of our sex-toy chest, off our insistence on four able limbs and two well-spaced eyes—it's messing with our dick AND our pussy, the most mistaken-for-sacred idols the world has ever known, so if we're scared, it is totally okay. We should be. I'm scared, *and* I have no idea what to wear to this shindig.

What I will do, however, is don some Capezios (the eighties ARE BACK, shut the hell up) and moonwalk (badly) out on the floor. You will slide out beside me, and take me for a dip and a spin. Then we'll all open-eye meditate with each other and watch with delight as our upper lips grow moustaches, then part and reveal full Marilyn mouths, pursed and sibilant, expressing a divine juice from a beyond-yonic mango in our foreheads, dripping down, coming on our eyelids, noses, and cheeks—all good nourishment in preparation for what's coming.

And what's coming is something only you and I can create—so let's make it with mercy, and compassion, and kindness, and beauty, and love. We're all of us going to need it.

A Drag Queen Born in a Female Body

Adrian Dalton (aka Lola Lypsinka)

interviewed by (photographer) Ashley [savageskin.co.uk]

Ashley: When did you first become aware of your feelings of gender dysphoria?

Adrian: I knew something wasn't quite right from an early age, but had no idea what. Had I been a masculine kind of child, it might have been more obvious to me and those around me just what the problem was. However, that wasn't the case; I was in no way a tomboy. I clearly recall the fact that I repeatedly asked Father Christmas for a tiara, just like the one I had seen Princess Diana wearing on TV. I was into Kylie Minogue music and make-up.

During my teens, I decided that I must be a lesbian as I was in a relationship with a girl. I looked very femme. I only consciously became aware of the true extent of my gender angst at the age of seventeen, when I first came to London, where I hoped to pursue a career in acting, singing, and modelling.

Ashley: So, how did those feelings manifest themselves?

Adrian: I finally became aware that I actually felt like a male who was trapped in a female body. However, I was still somewhat in denial and would not have admitted to anyone that I was transsexual. At the same time, I was becoming increasingly annoyed that people were looking at me and responding to me as if I were female, which was hardly surprising, since having been bullied at school, I had consciously created a super-feminine image in the hope that this might make people like and accept me. I wore loads and loads of make-up and tried to act in a very feminine manner, almost becoming someone I wasn't. I was constantly aware that when I was with my male friends I was putting on an act, albeit successfully, but I didn't like the fact that they responded to me as if I were female. That just wasn't me.

Ashley: When did you become involved in the gay scene?

Adrian: When I was seventeen. Initially I went because I assumed I was a lesbian, but I ended up just hanging out with other gay guys. I later became known by my friends as the crap lesbian, because I basically stopped fancying women entirely—which was a bit inconvenient, as I'd just come out! At the time I dressed very flamboyantly. I had long blonde hair and used to watch Marilyn Monroe and Brigitte Bardot films in order to emulate their mannerisms. In some ways I must have looked like a female impersonator. I felt like I was in disguise.

Ashley: You got a lot of attention from straight men. How did you cope with that?

Adrian: Some of my friends thought I was lucky. After all, from the age of around seventeen, I was attracted to guys, and straight men seemed to like the look I'd contrived. However, the attention I got from them was difficult to relate to. They were attracted to me because they saw me as female, which I knew I wasn't, so their attention disturbed and annoyed me. I didn't want to be treated like a girl; it felt emasculating. So I never had a relationship with a man when I was in a female body. I would not have dated a straight guy—the dynamic would have been all wrong. The guys I did like were other gay guys who obviously weren't interested in me as I was in a female body. So, I was kind of stuck. I didn't do relationships.

Ashley: When I first met you in 1997, you introduced yourself as Lola and told me that your image was inspired by your drag queen friends.

Adrian: At that time I became more aware on a conscious level that I felt like a gay man. I wasn't actually ready to come out and tell people, so my compromise was femme drag. I became even more over-the-top, wearing wigs, massive false eyelashes, tons of make-up, and vertiginous heels in the hope that I would pass as a drag queen. I christened myself Miss Lola.

Ashley: When did you actually decide to begin your transition, and what prompted that decision?

Adrian: All throughout my early to mid-twenties, the feeling that I was trapped in the wrong body became stronger and stronger, however hard I might try to suppress them. I did try my hardest to stay in the body with which I was born, but ultimately that proved to be impossible, as it would have involved denying my true self. I was drinking a lot. I am an alcoholic anyway and would probably have been so without my gender issues, but drinking did in many ways help me to block out some of the negative feelings I was having.

One of the catalysts that initiated my transition was hearing about FTM London, a support group for female-to-male transsexuals. This opened the door for me to meet others like me.

Surprisingly enough, hitting rock bottom with my alcoholism and going into recovery was another catalyst for change. Without the alcohol to mask my feelings, my gender dysphoria was intolerable and impossible to deny. I felt obliged to initiate a transition.

Ashley: You are a writer. Tell us about that.

Adrian: Well, I'm currently finishing up a re-work of a novel I wrote called "Inside Lindsey's Handbag." It's very light gay, fictional comedy. The main character is a drag queen hooker called Sofonda Cox! I'm also at the planning and development stages of an autobiography based on my transition. I'm calling this "Being Lola: The story of a gay male drag queen born in a female body."

Ashley: Let's now talk about your performance. How did that come about?

Adrian: I've always loved drag. When I saw my first drag act I was about seventeen. I was amazed. I thought, wow, that's exactly what I do, she's a camp man dressing up as an over-the-top woman. I instantly identified.

In some ways, even before I transitioned, I was doing drag, but it's only been during the last year that I have actually started performing as such. Before that I'd never actually thought that it was something I could realistically aspire to, what with being born into a female body and all! I'm on the Ugly Agency's books, so I get some things through that. Working as Lola Lypsinka is great. It's like I've come full circle from the days when I was doing femme drag and trying to pass as a drag queen. Now it's just what I do.

My first drag show was a lip-synching piss-take to Britney's "Gimme More," featuring me and my friend Travis, aka La Traviata. That show was performed at Duckie and Trannyshack. I've taken part in loads of Vogue Balls and other random bits and pieces and have really enjoyed participating and coming up with ideas for costumes. I have also joined drag Theatre Company 'The Drama Queens' and we perform regularly at the Black Cap in Camden Town, London. Recently I appeared in a documentary on Channel Five that followed some of my agency's models.

Last year David Hoyle interviewed me, and I did drag as his guest for the Gender Dysphoria night of Magazine at the Royal Vauxhall Tavern. That was a great experience. He's one of my favorite performance artists. I also think it's really important for me to talk about my experiences, so I do, whenever I'm asked. So many people don't know much about transmen or think that we are all ultra masculine and heterosexual. Don't get me wrong, I'm one of the most effeminate FTM's I know, and as a camp transman who does drag I'm definitely in the minority. But we do exist. Basically there is as broad a spectrum of transsexual men as there is of biological ones. I felt like I was the only one years ago, so if talking about my experiences helps even one other person like me not to feel so isolated it will be worth it. For this reason I was pleased to have the opportunity to tell my story and go on GMTV. Needless to say, I was also looking forward to meeting Lorraine Kelly, she was great.

I'm living a life I always wanted but never thought I could have. It's been quite a journey.

dual citizenship

Ahimsa Timoteo Bodhrán

I was born not to this village but that one.

> *i was born to the tribe of men, not women.*
> *but i was taken by them at a young age.*
> *and turned against them.*
> *or rather, they were turned against me.*
> *we are still healing this rift.*
> *i am still waiting, as are we all*
> *from the camp of women, for a warrior,*
> *messenger, to welcome me on home.*
> *and home, i'll come. without relinquishing*
> *my dual*
> *citizenship.*

I was born to the tribe of men, taken in by that of women, raised by the elders and sisters of that community. A different fire. Still it burns in me, and I await at the edge of the village, peering out over the fields, for a messenger, on foot, a warrior walking by night through the woods, listening for the crackle of our fire. I am not the first to rise, as our warrior women stand, armed, to see who is coming. I sit by the elders, the grandmothers, watching through smoke, through ember and flame, to see if he will know my name, the one I was called at birth, the one I have carried all these years in this pueblo. He emerges from brush, from flame, surveys the gathering, nods, shows he is of peace, warrior-strong true, but his battle for me, by me, is another day. Seen and seeing, he walks toward the fire to kneel on one foot and make offering, whisper prayers to the fire. I lick my lips, not for him, maybe, but because I realize there is a dryness in me I cannot name. He is the one who will name it. I wait for the whisper of his words against the drum of my ear, a clear flute singing in my throat. Elders watch, say nothing. Offer a few other things to the fire. They have barely raised their eyes to greet. He begins to talk, low, over the flames, to see if they will be heard, his words, his offering. He marks the birch as he walks by, a way to find his way back, if needed. If needed for him ever to return. He talks to the fire, to us, to those Ancestors gathered, to those still coming. He works, talks through the flames, they rising to snap with his words. He offers the names of his people, his life, the gods he worships, his path. He has come for me. I have been called home, from home, to home. I am of age now, thirties, learned my skills of fight and war, love and healing, hunt and gather. He has come to ask for me, not only for him, but for his people, once mine. To resurrect a bloodline, heal the rifts between our tribes. I look at my Elders. They do not look at me, speak towards the fire. They say it has been long time since he came to their people, that he is one of us now, that he cannot leave his obligations to the people, his tribe, the one he was adopted into, the fields, this fire, he cannot leave this fire. He cannot leave the braiding of the young girls' hair, cannot leave the songs he must teach them, the braiding of voices he must do, the braiding of twine and reed into the baskets that carry our people through his days. He is no longer of that people, they say. One of us, now. One of us, always. Born to us before, born to the wrong village, now his claimed. He was a gift to us from the Creator. It is here he shall remain. He was born here, reborn here, given a name, purpose, path, people. Clan and totem, tribe. What could this other people, across the way, offer him? Memories of a childhood that was not his? A family that did not want him? A brotherhood that did not know what to do with him? Some warriors, they say, discarding their most proud, most noble and strong, most wise. A wasteful people, they say. Raised him we have, they say. Ours, they say. I look towards fire, flame. Eyes misting wet. The truth of their words, my longing. To stay, to come be with him and learn their ways. I do not want to leave my women, I say. I do not want to leave this fire, I say. Your people, my people, did not want me, I say. He cries, tears. He has been many years in waiting. He remembers the day I was taken away and cried.

I am to go with him. We are to live in the middle between both camps, visiting both. We are to start, create a new village. And call it wholme.

We will take embers from both fires.

Trans-ing Gender: The Surgical Option

Mercedes Allen

"Have you had surgery yet?" The question is often asked as if Genital Reassignment Surgery (GRS) were the Only Logical Conclusion.™ GRS is revered as the Grail: the only fitting end to the trans quest. Yet in my experience, transition has been more a journey than a destination.

At the age of nineteen, I left home with next to nothing, facing the prospect of either doing sex work or living on minimum wage. Some people have the temperament to do sex work without being affected. I don't. I tried to transition at that time, only to have doctor after doctor give me horror stories, refuse to help, or say they didn't know where to refer me. When finally told that the surgery would cost between fifteen and twenty thousand dollars, plus thousands more for medical procedures like breast augmentation and electrolysis, I gave up and tried to live with what I was given.

I discovered that for many, including many transsexual persons, there are few acceptable excuses for remaining a "pre-operative" transsexual forever. There may be medical reasons why the surgery is too dangerous for a particular person. The predicted results may not be satisfying. Even financial straits might explain the choice. But in all of these cases, the understanding is that people in this situation are "incomplete" and would surely want the surgery if they could have it. I have even heard the opinion that a "real transsexual" would let nothing stand in the way. When I chose to pass up surgery, some in the community suggested that if I weren't "real" enough to "follow through," I needed to discontinue my hormone therapy immediately and go back to presenting as male.

I know I am real. The decision to keep "it"—the dangly bit and baggage that sabotaged my legal and social status as a woman—did not stem from a fear of surgery, nor from identifying as anything other than a woman. Rather, it grew out of my artistic and spiritual explorations.

An artist myself, I had just discovered the aesthetic beauty of the transfemale body. My appreciation of the transfemale body was not fetishistic or even sexual. The thought of being female (or transfemale) was not itself a turn-on, although whenever I imagined myself in any situation, sexual or otherwise, I had to picture myself as female. This is an important distinction to make because the theory of "autogynephilia" has misdirected some researchers to dismiss many trans women as fetishists (itself a misunderstood concept that invalidates by assuming unreality). Two years after starting Androcur, my body had become nearly non-orgasmic; yet on an artistic and emotive level, I kept seeing transfemininity as beautiful.

I had also developed a spiritual curiosity about the reason I was born male. Was it to call into question the societal assumptions ascribed to gender? To challenge absolutes? To learn new ways of thinking? As someone who is part Native, I was also curious about Two Spirit tradition and understanding how my ancestors lived without surgery as an option.

As I went farther into transition, the journey-not-destination concept remained at the heart of my soul-search. My journey hinged more on receptivity and reflection than on a checklist of official steps. The struggle I went through, the fear of exchanging the familiar for the unfamiliar, the subconscious fears, the "what ifs": these were my rite of passage into womanhood. Cisgender (non-transgender) women never stop learning their femininity (or their own latent masculinity); cisgender men likewise. How can we say that we've "arrived" at the flick of a scalpel? I'd hazard a guess that someone could conceivably go through the whole transition process and still not know what it is to be a woman, while another can live in the closet as a crossdresser and still come to realize the more important realities of womanhood.

I've been asked whether I identify as female or transsexual. I'm not entirely certain that they are mutually exclusive. I see human existence as being shaped by a combination of biological determination, social conditioning, and choice. My identity is intrinsically female; my history and upbringing are transsexual. I can't separate them, nor do I see cause to hide either part. I'm a woman with a trans history and with some residual trans aspects that will probably remain a part of my life as woman.

The trouble with placing a heavy emphasis on GRS as the "endpoint" of our transition is that it focuses on eliminating the ways in which my trans history informs my womanhood. We can become so intent on becoming wholly female or wholly male that we abandon, hide or feel ashamed of those things that make us truly unique.

Transgender people have wisdom and experience that our friends, family, and acquaintances never dreamed of. A woman can talk to her female-to-male (FTM) partner and know that he really does understand the beautification and competition crap that girls are fed when they are growing up. A man can trust that his MTF partner understands the ruthless repression of emotions that were imposed upon him through his youth, maybe enough to allow himself to be more emotionally vulnerable in front of her. Those of us who have lived in two genders have a front-row view of the battle of the sexes, with a vivid understanding of what hormones do to our moods, of how differently men and women are perceived and treated in public venues, of the pervasiveness of male privilege, of how different dating as male is from dating as female, even if the gender of attraction doesn't change. Those perspectives are hard-won. It would be a shame to bury them.

With a ruthlessly gendered world as our backdrop, the decision to keep "it" can become a badge of honor. A gender transition is one of the most difficult paths to tread. We've gone through the ritual. We've done the firewalk. We have the marks on the soles of our feet. While some are comfortable with covering up the burns and never telling anyone about the experience, we have earned the right to embrace some of the differences and take pride in them.

Easier said than done. Living non-operatively can have some serious repercussions. In many areas, legal protections for transsexuals don't exist. Correct documentation of gender is often impossible until a surgeon's letter is produced, leaving one open to being outed on every occasion that identification is called for. We are segregated by gender in many public settings, including homeless shelters, hospitals, and prisons, leaving open the possibility of institutionally sanctioned rape and abuse. Even public restroom use can be called into question. And people can react quite negatively to the discovery of transsexual status, even to the point of violence.

Some might contend that not having GRS when it's available is "accepting second best." Perhaps, but only by the same kind of logic my mother used when she asked me, "Why would you want to be a woman, when men have the upper hand in life?" Logically speaking, social pressures would suggest GRS in self-defense. However, it would seem to me that "second best" would be having major surgery to meet societal expectations and legal standards, when I already see myself as a woman.

Despite these reservations, GRS can be a medical necessity. Not every transsexual needs it, but for those who do, it is an absolute necessity. Where the need and driving desire exists, it becomes the pivotal point at which closure can be achieved and one can move forward in life. Certainly the realities of identification issues, citizenship, equality, safety, and acceptance mean that GRS affects lives in transformative ways that no other "elective cosmetic" procedure ever could. It can also be absolutely necessary for one's genitals to be in a comfortable configuration in order to be able to function sexually and even emotionally in relationships.

It was this latter point that caused me to reconsider my decision not to pursue Gender Reassignment Surgery. I had found a wonderful partner with whom I'd connected perfectly on every level. Yet I couldn't bring myself to use my current configuration in any sort of intimate way. The satisfaction of experiencing intimacy in the way in which I felt it was intended still eluded me. Ultimately, the cerebral acceptance of a penis as a part of me could not overcome the "squick" of discomfort and disturbance that was an ongoing barrier to physical intimacy. And so I decided that I would have surgery after all.

But that is my individual journey. I've known others whose negative feelings around their genitals have been tolerable, or even negligible. Expecting one experience to fit all is unreasonable, especially with something as profound and life-changing as Genital Reassignment Surgery. People's reasons for remaining "non-operative" are as varied as their experiences.

We've entered an age in which our diverse community is discovering that we have the freedom to define ourselves, which is both a blessing and a curse. In the years following Stonewall, anything "trans" was ejected from the queer movement; in the politically correct '80s, butches and femmes were ejected from lesbian culture. This kind of infighting can lead to bitter rifts that take decades to heal. GRS is one more way in which we've rigidly set up a hierarchy of trans accomplishment and put members of our own community down to validate our own identities.

While railing against the manufactured prerequisites of womanhood or manhood, we need to avoid manufacturing our own prerequisites. The non-operative journey and the objections to it illustrate just one area in which we need to open our thinking to other journeys while expecting that others respect our own.

I am the "I"

Sean Saifa Wall

ast Sunday night I sat nervously in the Recovery House living room, looking out at a capacity crowd. As an organizer and activist, I often give presentations on very charged topics related to race, gender, and other forms of oppression. Tonight, though, I would share some of the most intimate details about myself: what brought me into Sex and Love Addicts Anonymous. Like many who enter the rooms of S.L.A.A., I had a familiar story of anonymous sexual liaisons, obsessive relationships, and fears of intimacy. Like other accounts of addiction and compulsion, the story of my shame and isolation has opened a path of liberation and wholeness.

I learned that my body was different as a five-year-old, in the cloistered, pre-pubescent world of playing "house" and "doctor." My female playmates had perforations in their vaginas, while my parts were fused. Unlike other little girls, I could actually pee standing up, which shocked and intrigued my peers. As a child, I ran around the house bare-chested, reveling in this freedom until the weight of gender roles put me into barrettes and dresses. When I started to sprout breasts, my mother bought

107

me a bra and prepared me to enter womanhood. By middle school, every-body around me was talking about acne, dating, and sex.

I liked girls, but knew from early interactions that romance between two people of the same gender was prohibited. My body began to change as well, but this was not the same puberty my female friends were going through. My voice started to deepen, my shoulders broadened, and I could feel facial hair growing. At the same time, cramps would often leave me huddled in a fetal position on the floor for hours at a time.

When my mother found out, she took me to my pediatrician. In less than a month, I was in a surgical gown preparing for a "gonadectomy." When I asked the nurse what a gonadectomy was, he mentioned things like "testicular feminization syndrome," "undeveloped organs," "not ovaries or testes," "undescended," and "turning in place." I still didn't under-stand what those terms meant. Following the gonadectomy, I became very depressed and felt tired all the time. In addition to therapy, the doctors prescribed estrogen and progesterone, two female hormones. I never felt right on them, but my mother always made sure that I took them, remind-ing me how "beautiful" they would make me.

I managed to fit in among my high school classmates, despite the ever-present threat of homophobia. Low-income, black, and queer, I found hope in TV shows such as "In the Life" that featured gay content, and I enjoyed hanging out at the LGBT Center in the West Village. Although I projected an image of self-assuredness to my classmates, I wanted more than anything to to connect with other queer people, whether sexually or platonically, on the internet or in real life.

When I went away to college, I stopped taking the hormone supple-ments. My desire for connection remained, but fear got in the way of sex-ual encounters. I hooked up with people, but never got completely naked. This strategy worked until a woman showed interest in me during my junior year. Terrified by the thought of getting naked and having sex, I tearfully called my mom, whose sympathy was compounded by guilt and helplessness.

One night, I brought myself to type "testicular feminization syndrome" into a search engine and came across a website for women with Androgen Insensitivity Syndrome (AIS). The symptoms listed for AIS eerily answered all the questions I had about my body. Everything started to make sense at that point: the team of medical interns examining my body after the gonadectomy, the estrogen replacement therapy, and the many doctors who fingered my ass checking for a scrotum.

When I had learned that I was intersex, I brought this issue to my mother. She told me that I am one of at least seven people in my family born with AIS. This condition affects genetically male children who have varying, but limited responses to testosterone. Depending on a medically defined scale of femininity and masculinity, children are assigned a male or female identity. Given the appearance of my genitals at birth, I was assigned female.

I was relieved to know the truth at last, but I felt so much shame. All of these questions floated through my mind:

"Am I a man or a woman?"

"Why didn't doctors tell me the truth?"

"Who could love a freak like me?"

I became deathly afraid of sexual intimacy. My early sexual experiences were lessons in intersex anatomy. When the women I slept with asked about my genitals, they triggered memories of doctors and interns searching my body with prying eyes and fingers, seeking answers to the complexity of human nature. I had sex with these women, but I could not ask for what I wanted in the bedroom because I did not know. My body was as foreign to me as it was to them. I experienced my first orgasm only at the age of twenty-five, but when I finally did learn to pleasure myself, it became a drug that I sought day and night.

Several years later, I started to live as male. I did what seemed impossible: changed my name in the courts, started testosterone, and reclaimed my body and gender. Despite these victories, I started to spiral out of control in other areas of my life. My desire for queer connection and intimacy was now fueled by testosterone. I hooked up with people on the Internet, had an affair with a co-worker, and cheated on the woman I was dating. Ironically, the more sex I had, the more depleted I felt. My already low self-esteem plummeted. I needed help.

I found a therapist recommended by a co-worker. On the first visit he asked, "When did you realize that love was not possible?" I looked at him with tears in my eyes and answered a quivery, "I don't know." The only models of love relationships I had seen were marked by infidelity and abuse. I learned to put up emotional walls; I believed my worth was based on how good I was in bed or how selfless I was as a partner.

After our initial visit, he recommended that I check out S.L.A.A. I laughed. I wasn't an addict. I knew about addiction. My parents had struggled with addiction; I was different. I wasn't addicted to drugs or alcohol. But as I would come to discover, my drug was people, with whom sexual relations served as a proxy for my overwhelming need to belong.

When I entered recovery, I had been on testosterone for over three years and experienced some physical changes that enabled me to live as male. I felt validated when people recognized me as a man as opposed to seeing me as either a woman or some kind of freak. The last thing I wanted to talk about was my gender identity; I felt more comfortable, at group meetings, discussing twisted family dynamics and the daily struggle to maintain sobriety.

With the help of my therapist, I realized that hiding the complexity of what made me a man was only inhibiting my recovery and personal growth. After close to two years in the program, I told the group I was intersex. Despite my shame and extreme vulnerability, I felt that people genuinely saw me for who I was. More than letting them witness my trauma, I was giving them the opportunity to recognize my resilience.

I continue to come out publicly and privately as an intersex person despite people's misunderstandings. In seeking to convey the full scope of my life, I have realized that I am a hybrid of both sexes in ways that are unique and powerful. By attending S.L.A.A. meetings and pursuing recovery, I am reclaiming my life. By telling my story, I am reclaiming my voice as an intersex person. Those of us with intersex conditions and varying gender identities are the only ones who can know and tell our own stories.

make me a vessel for anomaly

simon iris

Call me boy.

sixteen years ago you would not have believed it; i am what i had never intended to be. there is this wildness in me, and they tell me, "say: 'call me boy.'" like "boy" will tame this unkempt spasticity and ferocity; like "boy" will mend the broken parts of me that fight tirelessly for the right to decay and die. like i will ever be this spoonfed whitebread maniacal joust at masculinized life, and like they would like it, anyway. they don't, and they wouldn't. they tell me i'm so strong and they say "boy" like i would want to hear it, and i wouldn't, and i don't. but they feel calm, convinced that this transition has ended, not fruitlessly; that this boy in me has emerged beautifully and fully grown, owning names and space like real estate, like it was theirs for me to take back to begin with.

there is this myth called boy that walks behind me.

one foot stays planted sometimes, and i rush to advance but he moves with me in circles. there are times i am sure you cannot distinguish a leader. sometimes i feel his breath on my neck, and i can hear them when they yell sir, and they are talking to me but they see him instead. i try and i try and i try to move away but he trails me, he prevails though i think i stand above his height, and homing in on he—my ever-constant shadow—they lose me and i become him.

there is this boy called myth that i could never be.

sometimes he hovers in front of me; i am bathed in his trailing effervescence, and there is something in him that i long for. in my hours of wanting, i cannot tell you where i end and he begins, where his mood shifts and becomes my demeanor careening untamed. when he is angry i am furious and when he is quiet i am stiff and cold. when he loves i am enamored with the world and mindlessly emancipated by the beating of his heart. i follow and they call me boy because i want to be strong.

they tell me, "say, 'call me man.'" like "man" matches this wild yearning for gender freedom; like raising castes and glasses to toast my newfound privilege marks achievement; like i don't grieve with every time i pass. feel a weighted void where my gender used to be. see my gender bleeding helplessly on the curb, kicked and downtrodden by odd words like "man" and crying for recognition; blundering down a hollow hallway saying, "call me nothing instead," and waiting to be released.

there is this girl that is not yet empty.

she was there and they loved her, but firm in her absence this rag-doll wild boy emerged and she and all her glory were left to flounder and fall into the fire of sheer memory. and now they call me girl. lips curl and grin with sinful pleasure in having wronged me, robbed me of the prize of masculinity, and i wonder where they put she in me and when she will be allowed to enjoy his femininity. she will perspire under the flame of interrogation and question her home in me, and they will say, "tell them, 'that was never me.'" but i flinch and hear her calling and flinch and feel her tugging at my sleeve and flinch and she is suddenly in me and i wonder if it would be more simple to remove my skin from the equation and let her bleed my history. she is a mountain of accidents and simple requests and she is only waiting for her avalanche.

there is something like a story.

they will never eradicate from me this need to create, and i want to show them what i could do if they would release my hands from the stocks of my body. show them butch like i mean it and stone like i've lived it and survivor to the ends of the earth—i earned this wounded grin and spinning prism of names. i will dance for the love of dancing like i embrace gender for the love of bending bodies and words into something i can call restitution and remedy, and make my he a being strong in his arbitrary divinity.

there is a constant fragility in his awareness of who he was, and where she is, and the knowledge that they are bound forever with rope tighter than any knot he could tie around wrists and ankles and necks craned to see him when she is at his most dominant, or cloth tied across her eyes when all he wants to do is forget. i am wandering barefoot through broken territory.

there is a restlessness in me.

like the crashing of waves on shorelines and he wants to know when she will have the spotlight again. he moves in between her and she will discover new places in me to rest and grow.

there is a breathless reprieve.

she will hold herself in his hand and ask quietly what it means.

make me a vessel for anomaly.

i will find refuge in the spaces between.

call me genesis.

she is born. he is here.

i am rising.

I am Transreal: a reflection on/of *Becoming Dragon*

Micha Cárdenas

Becoming Dragon *was a Mixed-Reality Performance which questioned the one-year requirement of "Real Life Experience" that transgender people must fulfill in order to receive Gender Confirmation Surgery, and asked if this could be replaced by one year of "Second Life Experience" to lead to Species Reassignment Surgery. For the performance, Micha Cárdenas lived for 365 hours immersed in the online three-dimensional environment of Second Life with a head mounted display, only seeing the physical world through a video feed, and used a motion capture system to map her movements into Second Life. The installation included a stereoscopic projection for the audience. A Puredata patch was used to process her voice to create a virtual dragon's voice. During the year of research and development of this project, Cárdenas began her real-life hormone replacement therapy and wrote poetry and prose about the experience which was included in the performance. The project was realized through a collaboration between Cárdenas, Christopher Head, Elle Mehrmand, Kael Greco, Ben Lotan, and Anna Storelli. More documentation of the performance is at secondloop.wordpress.com.*

I am transreal. Look at me. When you do, a million iridescent scales across my dragonhide flick, move, and align to create a multiplicity of perceptions, transversal illusions, and realities cutting through each other, intersecting, dancing. Look at me. You see a shimmering of my fantasies and yours, a convergence of your minute sensory events, your imaginary constructs and my desires. Look at me. The mythopoetic elements of your reality and mine come into contact, unwind, and become a recombinant event of male and female and something else, something more, for just an instant. Perhaps after that initial instant, one of your myths takes over your perception and you decide that you understand, but before that, I instill confusion and doubt. I can see it on your face.

I am becoming a shapeshifting creature of legend, a dragon. Standing here on the border, the sunlight through the clouds defeating the fence, I am transreal, between realities, moving through layers of the symbolic, the imaginary, and the real. Simultaneously quivering, swapping out, and swapping back in, I move too fast for anyone to discern the border between them. I am existing between my fantasies and desires, which are driving the changing form of my body, and which also drive the moment of perception in which you see me and call me ma'am, sir, dude, miss, or avoid choosing a category. Speaking, being with different people throughout the day, my body and name changes, my realness or unrealness oscillates. You see me standing here, but really you see my avatar, my body, which is under construction. We bring our illusions together. You see soft skin. I see the pills and the bloody razor that made it soft, making me feel happier, more feminine. You see scales, I see textured prisms and their glow values as created through my software.

A dark moment in the street at night: your illusions of masculinity swirl up against the confusion I instill in you, and you attack. My reality becomes a blur, a flurry of motion, and a sharp chemical emotional reaction as I strike back with pressurized chemical weapons. Yet even in that moment, I am transreal, between my reality and yours, finding only a wide fissure between the two.

In bed together, my lover and I are transreal, deep in our illusions of each other, feeling our very real emotions for each other, between bodies, looking into her eyes, slipping out of myself and my concerns and into the bright nebula of pleasure.

I am *becoming something else*. In this moment, this being-in-transition, I am willfully stepping into the unknown. I am between realities. I can imagine what I want to become and then choose to become that new thing, but it is radically ungraspable, inconceivable. I can never know the reality of what I am choosing to become, desiring to become. My decision to transform can never be the right one, because it is always based on an illusion: a fantasy, a false model with only a few points of data, not the rich details of an embodied life. As the transformation unfolds, those unknown events begin to occur—seeing my breasts in the mirror for the first time after shaving my chest closely; feeling the movement in my orgasm change into something new; or just walking down the street for a moment as a girl, unnoticed and not needing any special attention. My decision to *become something else* is always a decision to become mythopoetic, because the reality of the new state is always unknown, imaginary, a construct, a fantasy.

Yet I don't seek to decry this radical state of uncertainty; I seek to embrace it. The very moments of everyday perception are also intersections of a real materiality with my symbolic and imaginary processing engines making sense of them, down to the way that I understand what pleasure is and what pain is and when the two become so close as to be indistinguishable. And a choice not to transform is of course still a choice to transform into a different state, as our bodies are all in permanent transition, aging, training, consuming, producing, perceiving, creating new folds in our craniums.

Through this process, I am also becoming an artist. Yet this is simply another fantasy which I use to structure my desires and find direction. Artist, porn star, student, professor, father, mother, husband, wife, lover, child, priest: these are all simply performances of being. Yet their being a performance makes them neither less real nor more real: just another fold in the swirling interplay, the kaleidoscope of realities that is our being.

A mixed-reality performance using an online 3D virtual world simply highlights the fantasy nature of our everyday interactions, of the physical world, by referring back to the physical, stirring up our memories and conceptions of embodiment. "Mixed-reality performance" is a misnomer, as every step of our waking lives is a mix of realities: our self-perceptions, muscle memory, proprioceptions; others' perceptions of us, our perceptions of their perceptions of us as they look at us, or don't; our understanding that we are walking, taking a step, on a sidewalk, beside a building. A mixed-reality performance simply highlights this fact, or this fiction, and allows one to see and begin to question the structure of reality. I embrace the pleasure of bits projected on my skin and the flickering of digital lights in my eyes, of the simulacrum of my own fantasy which creates that same fantasy. The mixture of real and imaginary is more real for being mixed. While one can draw one's fantasy, or write it out in words, three-dimensional virtual worlds bring us one step closer to seeing in front of our eyes the fantasy films which play behind our eyes; yet many more steps remain to bring us closer to dreams. In my dreams I smell, I feel my body in action, I have visceral emotions. Software such as Second Life is far from emulating such unreal realities. Still, we can make steps closer to dreams, with motion capture, head mounted displays, tactile interfaces, wish pressure interfaces. I wish for another reality: the electricity on my skin changes, transferring the new desired location to the system, and the pressure interface responds, as my chair morphs from a car seat to a comfy recliner in my skybox . . . loading world . . . arriving.

The mixture of realities we can willfully create is swirling, changing colors, deepening, almost ready to imbibe. Today we can become, in our minds and at a low resolution, any creature we wish. Through nanobiotech and soon through body hacking, perhaps the dream of shapeshifting, of becoming bird, wolf, or dragon, is rapidly approaching. We need only to shed our fantasy of being real, to find the courage to embrace the magic in our hands.

Our identities are shifting, a daily act of creation, permanent transition. With these new identities, we become inoperative, incompatible with the protocols of heteronormative structures. The need, then, is to extend these identities, amplify their possibilities, take them off of the screens—beyond media, into our bodies and daily lives—through new practices of mixed-reality, Tactical Biopolitics, and Science of the Oppressed, following the trajectory of Technologies of Transformation. The possibilities have been opened for making new images, new objects, new models of identity together in immersive shared three-dimensional spaces. With *Becoming Dragon*, I sought to go farther, to bring the body into the new space of expression, to become the body in transmission, performing a flickering digital shapeshifter. At first my physical body rebelled, but after six days, I began to acclimate to this new networked somatic architecture, this being-across-realities, transreal identity. The possibilities have only been just touched upon, the doorway barely cracked. Mixed-reality performance can serve as a liminal space of training, creation, and development for new unimagined assemblages of desire, resistance, and becoming. Yet my voice, however modified, still belies my gender, challenges me. Perhaps the current technologies are best suited to training the body. I fail, the technology fails, crashes, pushed to its limits. The world goes black, scrolling text while I wait for the reboot.

To me, being transgender is so much about the hope of change, of transformation. While political posters promise change, I hope for a change no president can create. As long as we have been human, we have also been dog, wolf, bear, snake, cat, goddess, spirit, tree. Perhaps in the trans longing to become something else, one can see the deep desire for connection and transformation, the age-old longing to become more than we are. Perhaps with the unfolding of new technologies of transformation, we can shake off the regimes of government, religion, and science which seek to define and limit us and tell us that we are only what we are now. At the root of my performance and at the beginning of action is the hope for the possibility of another world. Along with an acceptance of uncertainty that we can never truly know the outcome of our actions, we act with the hope that our actions will make our lives, and those of others, better than they are today.

Taking up Space

Kyle Lukoff

The hardest part about being hospitalized for an eating disorder was finding a hospital that would take me. It took weeks of phone calls, weeks of being told "Our program doesn't accept men," until I finally found one that was willing to have an FTM patient.

After I got to the hospital, the hardest part was figuring out how to tell the other patients that I was transsexual. After a day or so I went to the director of the clinic, figuring he would have some ideas about the best way to disclose to the group. Apparently he and the rest of the staff had discussed my "special case," and they had come to the unilateral decision that I should keep my identity as trans a secret. Or, as he put it, I "shouldn't bring outside issues into the group." He considered my transition irrelevant. Or, as he put it, "What does this have to do with eating disorder treatment?"

I didn't have an answer for him then, but I do now.

My gender directly fed my eating disorder. Or starved it, since I was anorexic rather than a compulsive eater. I didn't like my breasts or my hips or my stomach, and the thinner I got, the easier it was to bind my chest flat. My hips got narrower and my face got more angular, though since I was also on testosterone it's hard to parse out which changes came from what. When I talk about these two aspects of my identity, I often get a "well, duh" response. Starving away the parts of my body I'm uncomfortable with does make a certain amount of sick sense.

Still, I think that's too simple an answer. Eating disorders are extremely complex, and so am I.

Another explanation could be the commonest analysis of anorexics: a need for control. When my eating disorder resurfaced, my life and my gender were both undefinable. While I loved testosterone and the effects it had on me, it was also a challenge to go from a recognized gender to something in between. While I didn't *like* being read as female, it was at least predictable and understandable. But after about three months on T, I was passing some of the time but not all of the time. I was never sure which bathroom to use, or which customers at work were going to call me "Sir" or "Ma'am." My relationship with my parents had gone from strained to worse after my father told me that he already had a son and didn't want another. I was in an emotionally abusive relationship, preparing to leave for law school, and on top of all that, I was going through a second puberty. Almost unconsciously I began to cut back on how much I was eating per day. I started to treasure the feeling of hunger in the pit of my stomach and the way it took my mind off everything else.

As I started to lose weight I found that I liked it. I liked the feeling of control I had over my body and my personal habits. I began restricting more consciously. Early on in physical transition, I felt as if my understanding of my body was slipping. All I had heard from other FTMs was that testosterone was a good thing: it would cure me, would mold my pounds of flesh into something that I could cherish. Instead, what happened was that my familiar-yet-feared body was changing in ways that I wanted but didn't expect. Any control at all that I could exert over myself helped quell my fear that my body was suddenly turning not only unfamiliar but also unmanageable. Being hyper-vigilant about food made me feel like at least one aspect of my personal appearance was under my own jurisdiction, that I had a choice in the matter, that not everything revolved around the presence or absence of testosterone in my system.

It didn't help that the T ramped up my metabolism. Suddenly I had to eat twice as much just to feel satisfied. After years of disordered eating habits, this rapid acceleration of hunger wrecked the uneasy peace I had reached with my appetite. I became terrified of gaining weight. It wasn't so much about being fat; I identify as a fat ally, and understand that sizeism is intertwined with and related to other forms of oppression. Paradoxically, it was the body-positive arguments that made me want to lose weight. Fat positivity is partially about reclaiming space, and being proud of the space that one takes up. As much as I agreed with these politics intellectually, they never resonated emotionally. Internally, I shied away from this rhetoric because for my whole life I've wanted to take up as little space as possible.

It's no wonder eating disorders are rampant among women. Women are conditioned to take up as little space as possible in the world. Physically, women are expected to cross their legs at the knee and ankle. Women who sit with their legs comfortably apart or have a wide stance are considered masculine and aggressive. The ideal woman is slender, with breasts large enough to keep her from looking male but small enough to save her from appearing wanton and sexually abundant. She must always be on a diet but should never, ever admit to being hungry. She must take care to not take up more room than she deserves.

When I identified as a girl and woman, I could never keep up with this image. Of course I couldn't; it's an idea created and propagated by glossy magazines and patriarchal impulses, one that simultaneously puts women on a pedestal and leaves them in the trash heap. My mother raised me to have confidence and assertiveness, important qualities in girls, but I lacked some essential grounding in myself. I fled to traditional trappings of femininity, eye shadow and skirts, hoping that I could somehow train myself to be a girl, that I could learn how to grow into a woman. Above all, I wanted to lose weight, believing that somehow a loss of five, ten, or maybe fifteen pounds would soothe the discomfort I felt being present in my own skin.

I've always felt like I was too much. Too emotional, too passionate, too smart, too eccentric. And constantly hungry. Growing up, I thought that if I could curb my appetite, I would also curb those feelings that I wasn't quite right, that something inside me didn't match my outside. I hoped that if there were less of me, there would be less of me that felt wrong.

In my late adolescence I came out as queer, and I also came into a political consciousness that actively questioned patriarchal ideas of femininity and womanhood. I read *The Beauty Myth* and *Body Outlaws*, and saw in myself the ways that people who are assigned female at birth are oppressed by gender policing. I stopped feeling compelled to wear eye makeup and floral skirts and began experimenting with male drag and buzzcuts. I wore mascara sometimes, nail polish sometimes, lip gloss sometimes, but only when I felt like it, not because I felt like I had to.

I wish I could say that this was when I stopped trying to lose weight, but that would be a lie. As I discovered more about myself, I also discovered that my very existence was contested by millions around the country, many in my high school, and even a few in my own family. Lesbians and gay men are subject to enough harassment and oppression, and I didn't even fit into a nice mainstream *Will and Grace* image of homosexuality. I began experimenting with sadomasochism, a practice that is still considered a mental illness by the American Psychiatric Association. I explored polyamory in a time when same-sex marriage is a big enough step. And then I came out as transgendered.

In retrospect, it's not surprising that my eating disorder spiraled out of control when I began to transition physically. Trans folk are told we do not and should not exist, and when we do exist we must make every effort to assimilate. Our existence is often a shadowy one, living as we do in the cracks between bureaucracies and regulations, with mismatched identification and uncertain legal status. Sometimes I wonder if my anorexia resurfaced as an unconscious surrender to these oppressions: Did I buckle under the pressure of a world telling me I had no place in it? Was I trying to disappear? It wouldn't have been the first time.

By the time I was hospitalized as a twenty-three-year-old man, I was wearing the same pants size that I wore in middle school: a size zero in women's. For years before this, I had raged against the very idea of women's size zero, against the implication that the ideal woman is one who has completely disappeared. I preferred men's clothing, I claimed, because its sizes accurately reflected the amount of space one took up in the world.

Despite the rhetoric, I loved being a size zero in junior high. I was a girl small in stature. I tried to hide within myself, but all too often my big mouth gave me away. I had hoped that being short and skinny would make me less odd, less noticeably an outcast. It always felt like all sixty, seventy, eighty pounds of me was just too much for the world to handle.

Years later, when my weight dipped back down, I was trying to hide again, from myself this time. I was scared, and unhappy, and uncertain, and in pain. I thought that if there were less of me there would be less of those feelings, too. I thought I could starve away all the hurt, that emotional pain could be replaced by physical pain. That the size zero jeans I fit into would somehow turn me into a zero, a nothing, a happy, carefree blank. By the time I was hospitalized I thought that treatment was my only salvation, that I would enter an anorexic and exit a whole person, comfortable with his emotions and happy with his size.

That didn't happen either. I had hoped that being hospitalized would cure me, would provide me with the tools I needed to thrive in a world that barely acknowledges my existence. Instead, when the director of the eating-disorders ward told me not to disclose, I shut up. I ate my "therapeutic snack" and participated in yoga, drew an ouroboros in art therapy, and didn't talk much about the eating disorder that landed me there. Instead I learned that recovery ultimately comes from the inside. No hospital in the world could cure me while I still believed that I didn't deserve to exist, that I was a size zero in waist and in soul. This is a lesson I'm still learning and will be learning for a long time.

Almost exactly two years after hospitalization, I'm back up to a size 30 in men's pants. I'm still "too much" in a lot of ways: emotional, loudmouthed, opinionated, and extreme. But instead of starving away my feelings, instead of trying to shrink down to nothing, I'm going to therapy, spending time with friends, writing, and figuring out my way in the world as a man. I am more comfortable with my body and how it relates to others, whether I'm having a one-night stand or cuddling with a friend. I am working at a job that uses both my intellectual and physical strength. I am navigating my path through the world from inside my body instead of pretending I don't have a body at all. I am a perverted queer, a gender-radical transsexual, a feminist, an ally, and an outlaw. And now I know that people like that deserve as much space as we can claim.

Transliteration

Francisco Fernández

A veces me cuesta describir mi identidad en distintos idiomas y a la vez mantener alguna coherencia. La primera vez que leí acerca de géneros no tradicionales fue en internet, donde el inglés es el idioma dominante; así encontré conceptos como *transgender* y *genderqueer* con los que me sentí identificado enseguida. Las personas que escribieron ese contenido en la red pueden servirse de esas palabras en su vida cotidiana, pero yo vivo en Argentina; ¿cómo adaptarlas a mi entorno? Podría usar directamente las palabras inglesas, lo que me haría sentir colonizado; o podría usar la palabra española "transexual," que no me describe satisfactoriamente. Elegí una tercera opción: apagar mi computadora y buscar gente trans de por acá.

A través de grupos de apoyo, charlas y revistas, encontré una rica tradición trans que incluye el movimiento travesti. Antes sólo había escuchado la palabra "travesti" como peyorativo, pero descubrí que algunas personas se la habían reapropiado para darle ellas mismas un nuevo sentido. Es imposible dar una definición precisa que abarque a todas las travestis, pero en general son personas que al nacer fueron declaradas varones, y que tienen una identidad femenina y/o de mujer. Consideré usar el término para mí mismo; nunca conocí a nadie transmasculino que lo utilizara, pero tenía cierto sentido. Sin embargo, no sentía que yo tuviera derecho a apropiarme de un término que jamás fue usado en mi contra. Además, encontré una palabra más adecuada: "transgénero."

"Transgénero" tiene las mismas raíces etimológicas que *transgender*, y a veces se usa con el mismo significado, pero también se suele usar con el sentido de "trascender el género." Es decir que es similar a *genderqueer*—un género *queer* o no heteronormativo—pero su significado surgió entre hispanohablantes, y no como una traducción literal de *transgender*; eso me agrada. La única desventaja es que la mayoría de las personas jamás escucharon la palabra transgénero. Cuando empecé a descubrir y construir mi identidad, eso no importaba mucho, pero ahora quiero poder expresar—en términos comprensibles—cómo entiendo mi propia existencia. Puedo tratar de explicar el concepto de transgénero, o usar la palabra transexual por pragmatismo. No es una elección simple, porque a veces hasta "transexual" causa confusión acerca de cuál es mi identidad. En esas situaciones, trato de explicar mi género desde cero. Esta opción también presenta dificultades:

Soy un chico. Un chico que nació nena. No, eso es mentira. No nací nena, al igual que no nací con un nombre—ambas etiquetas me fueron colocadas por otras personas. Quizás debería decir que soy un chico que nació con el cuerpo de una chica. Pero, ¿tenía realmente el cuerpo de una chica? No tenía caderas anchas, ni pechos. Una vez me preguntaron si había nacido con tetas; la verdad es que no conozco a nadie que haya nacido con tetas. Bueno, entonces podemos decir que soy un niño que

nació con genitales de niña. ¿Genitales de quién? ¿De una niña?
¡De ninguna manera! Eran mis genitales—por lo tanto, geni-
tales de nene. Entonces, soy un chico con genitales de chico.
(También soy un chico con dedos de chico y rodillas de chico—
no sé por qué nunca me preguntan por todo eso.) En resumen,
soy un niño con cuerpo de niño, y por eso soy trans.

Eso no aclara mucho, ¿no? Sin embargo, me gusta usar partes de esa respuesta cuando alguien me pregunta por mi sexo. *Hay una diferencia entre género y sexo,* me dicen a veces. *Entiendo que seas un chico, pero ¿tu sexo es masculino o femenino?* Esperá—¿no acabas de decir que el género no es lo mismo que el sexo? ¿Entonces por qué le estás atribuyendo un género al sexo, llamándolo masculino o femenino? O ni siquiera un género, porque la masculinidad y feminidad no tienen necesariamente que ver con ser hombre, mujer, u otra cosa. Por ejemplo, yo soy varón, pero bastante femenino. ¿Eso me hace del sexo femenino? Si me desnudo e imito a James Dean, ¿me vuelvo del sexo masculino? La masculinidad y la feminidad son como las normas del género—las reglas para ser un "buen" hombre o una "buena" mujer—pero ¿cuántos de esas normas podemos cumplir cuando estamos desnudos?

Me parece que el lenguaje crea una confusión formidable de cuerpos y géneros, y no es un problema exclusivo del español: también ocurre, por ejemplo, en inglés y francés. Este desorden no es necesariamente negativo: genera la posibilidad de buscar caminos alternativos. Para mí, ser consciente de este caos es liberador porque significa que cualquier identidad que elija va a ser tan coherente o incoherente como las otras. En vez de buscar respuestas en los binomios—varón/mujer, feminidad/masculinidad, sexo/género—decidí reclamar mi cuerpo para mí mismo, para darle forma y amarlo, vestirlo y moverlo. Sobre todo, para nombrarlo.

Si me esforcé tanto en encontrar palabras para describirme, es porque el idioma cumple un rol importante en crear—o encontrar—quiénes somos. Ustedes, mis geniales *queers*, y no-*queers*—geniales *personas*—seguro que lo entienden: Hay una fuerza impresionante en el acto de autodeterminación. Para mí, nombrarme tiene el objetivo de crear un lugar en la gran galaxia del género donde me sienta como en casa, y deja abierta la posibilidad de mudarme cuando sea necesario. Ahora mismo soy un chico, pero pronto voy a levantar campamento y dirigirme hacia la hombría. Aún mientras recorro el camino de nena a nene, ya me estoy preparando para aquel cambio de género.

S ometimes I find it hard to describe my identity across languages. I first read about non-traditional genders through the internet, where most content is in English; that's how I came across concepts like transgender and genderqueer, which resonated with me immediately. I am from, and live in, Argentina; how should I translate those ideas into my daily life? I could use the English words, which would leave me feeling culturally colonized, or I could use common Spanish terms like "*transexual*," which didn't describe me accurately. I chose a third option: turn off my computer and go find the local trans community.

Through support groups, talks, and presentations, I encountered a rich trans tradition, such as the *travesti* movement—a group of people who reclaimed the word for "transvestite." *Travestis* are usually people who were assigned male at birth, and who identify with femininity and/or womanhood. I considered using it for myself, although I've never met a guy who identifies as *travesti*. It might be fun to mix things up that way, but I found a term which was even more appropriate: *transgénero*.

Transgénero translates directly as "transgender" but is often used to mean "transcending the gender binary." It's a concept very similar to genderqueer, and I enjoy the fact that it was developed here. There's one drawback: Most people have never heard of it. At the beginning of my self-construction that didn't matter much, but now I want to translate, in a way comprehensible to others, how I understand my own existence. I can either try to explain the term *transgénero*, or define myself as "trans-sexual" for the sake of communication. It's a tough choice. And when all words seem to fail, I try to explain my gender from square one. Here's one attempt:

> *"I am a boy. A boy who was born a girl. No, that can't be right. I wasn't born a girl any more than I was born with a name—both labels were stuck onto me by others. Maybe I should say that I'm a boy who was born with a girl's body. But did I have a girl's body at that point? I didn't have hips or breasts yet. Someone once asked me if I had been born with boobs, but I haven't met anyone who was born with breasts. All right then, I'm a boy who was born with a girl's genitalia. A girl's genitalia? Nuh-uh! They were definitely my genitalia—thus, a boy's genitalia. That would make me a boy with boy parts. (I'm also a boy with boy toes and knees—I wonder why no one ever asks me about those.) Yes, I'm a boy with boy parts, so that makes me trans."*

Not very illuminating, is it? Still, I like using parts of that answer when someone asks me about my sex. "Gender and sex are separate," they might say; "I understand that you're a boy, but is your sex male or female?" Wait a moment—didn't you just say that sex and gender are two different things? Then why are you gendering sex by using "male" and "female" to describe genitalia? Maybe we're sexing gender when we use those same words—male and female—to describe pronouns, or when we say "I identify as male."

In any case, we're making a huge messy mix of bodies and genders. This isn't necessarily undesirable—there's fun to be had in confusion and disarray. If my gender is "boy" and my organs are "female" and my pronouns are "male," then what am I? For me, being aware of this chaos is freeing. I am capable of creating my own genderful mess, thank you very much. Instead of looking to the binaries for answers—male/female, femininity/masculinity, sex/gender—I've decided to take my body back for myself—for me to shape, show off, love and dress and play. But above all, for me to name.

If I've gone to such lengths to find words for myself, it's because language is so important in creating—or finding—ourselves. You wonderful queers—and non-queers—you wonderful *people*—probably understand. There's a breathtaking power in self-determination. For me, naming myself is about creating a space where I can feel at home in the gender galaxy. And it's about being able to switch places as often as I need to. Right now I'm a boy, but soon I might pack my things and move to manhood. In my ongoing development from girl to boy, I'm also getting ready for *that* gender transition.

interlude

She says,

Us queers, we have to write our own scripts. Make your characters how you want them. Laugh when they surprise you. Smile when they shirk you, smirk when they avert eye contact. It's ok to sleep with someone who doesn't understand you—few people will—

watch how they love themselves; that's how they will love you.

Never settle for baggy pants when you feel like showin' off your ass. Never let a second glance keep you from that nail polish. Be patient. You can adore a body to dance just as easily as it's been numbed and discarded, but it takes time. Be resolute.

Take comfort in creating chaos,
and know that we thank you.

—Kris Gebhardt

. . . which is why I'm as cute as I happen to be.

———⊱✦⊰———

Part Three

Daddy Gets the Big Piece of Chicken

Fran Varian

He has no idea who I am. When I excuse myself from our table at the hipster sushi joint and turn toward the restroom, I can tell that he notices. His suit is expensive, his dinner is expensive; the top shelf sake he is pouring down his throat costs more than my entire outfit, but he doesn't know that. He works in finance, or in sales, and he earns more money than he is worth. He is drunk and he is staring at me. Hard. He is hard and he is transparent.

I walk slowly toward him. I understand the way my short black dress hugs my body. I understand that my shoes and my seamed stockings insinuate a garter belt, and that my red lips and the gardenia in my hair are exotic to him. I am bigger than the women he is with but not a damn one of them can walk the way I walk and I know that he knows that. He licks his lips: he is so very, very transparent.

I stop at his table and for the first time he looks me in the eyes. The smirk drops from his face. I know what he thinks I am. I know that he walks through the world assuming beautiful things like me are his for the taking. I have seen him and worked for him and serviced him a thousand times over. His dinner companions shift in their seats, especially his date who has convincingly pretended to not notice him ogling me for the past ten minutes. Someone clears their throat, and somewhere in the dank, drunken haze of his consciousness he remembers who the hell he is—or who he thinks he is. "Why don't you have a seat, sweetheart? You seem like you have something you want to say to me . . . ."

I smile, very slowly, and crouch so that I am resting solely on the balls of my feet, so that the hem of my dress rides up and the sacred place on my upper thigh where stocking meets flesh is exposed. I run my hand slowly up his arm, tracing the exquisite fibers of his suit jacket. I stop at the elbow and look into his slightly amused and slightly concerned face. I do have some-thing to say. I have had something to say to him for close to thirty years now and so I wrap my hand around his arm and bring my lips close to his face. I am quiet but every syllable is deliberately served to him while I squeeze his arm firmly and smile with my eyes: *"I am not your fucking girl."*

This is not my most mature moment, but it has been a long time coming. When I return to you at our table you are smiling too. "Dammit, honey. I don't want to have to fight anyone tonight. But I know that you are pleased. I can see it in the way you shift up in your chair, the way you take my hand in yours and run your thumb softly over my wrist. You just can't help yourself, can you?" But you know who I am, and you know the answer to that question.

We have saved for weeks to be able to afford this date. Many hours ago I ran a hot bath and added two pounds of Epsom Salts and some lav-ender. The salts are to help keep my rapidly deteriorating spine and hips somewhat placated in the impossibly hot shoes I have picked out for you; the lavender, because you love the way it smells on my skin. With tremen-dous precision I removed all of the hair from my legs, my underarms, and all the delicate places you might want to run your fingers or tongue over later. I scrubbed my skin fresh and soft for you and then I sealed it all with the coconut lotion you bought for me as a gift.

Before I ran that bath I stopped at the florist asking for a gardenia. I carried the frosty box home and placed it in the refrigerator, imagining its scent later inviting you to kiss me, imagining you closing your eyes and inhaling. I want you to pull that flower from my hair and put it in a bowl of water beside your bed before you undress and claim me. I want to wake up in the morning tangled in your arms and in the impossibly sweet smell of what we have done.

You were at home getting ready. I ran my hand through my stockings, carefully inspecting for runs, while you shaved in the bathroom mirror. In the bra and panties I set aside especially for this night, I curled my hair while you were considering which cock you would wear: as important a choice as which tie or which shoes. There are secret paths we walk that begin and end where language cannot exist. There are entire languages we wear on our bodies, only for each other, even when doing so endangers us. We wear these soundless words even though "they" will flub the translation and insist that we are poorly written.

I am writing this for you because I am your girl and this is how I love you.

When I was four years old I received a collection of plastic gem rings for Christmas. An entire fake-velvet-lined box of fake diamonds and emeralds and sapphires. It is significant to this narrative for you to understand that I fundamentally believed they made me a princess. I am the only child of two older, working-class parents. My father was forty-nine when I was born and he thought he would never have a child. He was always happy to acquiesce whenever I sauntered up to him holding out a tiny hand full of plastic saying: "Kiss it, Daddy! I am a princess." Like many foolish royals before me I squandered my wealth and by the following spring my only remaining gem was the ruby. The ruby had always been my favorite, which is why I hadn't lost it sooner. But then the terrible day came, the day I wore my ruby to Shop Rite with my Dad and I lost it. I wept the way any careless fool would weep when she realizes she has forever lost something she loves. My father—then in his fifties—was working close to one hundred hours a week to support my mother and me on a custodian's salary. He rarely slept more than four hours a day. He dropped to his knees as though I were actually the princess of something and began to frantically search the ground for my ring.

I am writing this for him.

Growing up, I rarely got the chance to eat with my father because he worked so much of the time. No matter what or when we ate, there was an unspoken rule in my family which was never questioned and from which we never deviated: Daddy got the biggest piece of chicken, or the biggest pork chop, or the biggest slice of meat loaf. Always. It made sense at the time, and it still does: Anyone doing that much physical labor needs to be fed. We are not the first or last working-poor family to adhere to the tradition of feeding the Daddy out of necessity. What I could not understand then was that we were also feeding him out of love and respect. Because my father was born in 1927, my sense of who he was compared to my friends' fathers or stepfathers was always different. My mother would explain to me that men of my father's generation, working-class men, had a different work ethic, a different sense of pride in relation to providing for their families. My father did not want my mother to work outside of the home; he wanted her to raise me, full-time. Clearly this is an enormous generalization. But even as a small child I could see the way my father's masculinity functioned to hold me up to the world and display me as something sacred.

Decades later, with a minor in Women's Studies under my belt, I know how heteronormative and sexist that may seem if you don't speak our language. *I am not writing this for you.* My father is the first person who taught me that masculinity is a construct. I knew it because he was different. He was strong, but not cocky. He was quiet, but relentlessly demonstrative of his love via his actions. He was a janitor. He was a courier. He was a school bus driver. He put meat on the table by servicing the needs of other people, people who often did not understand him or respect him. People who looked right through him and never said please or thank you. He did not complain, not even when his sobbing four-year-old robbed him of a solid hour of sleep by losing her plastic toy.

After dinner we leave the restaurant and you take my hand in yours. You walk on the outside, closest to the street. You do this because we are moving targets, even in San Francisco. You do this because you have been attacked for the masculinity you have constructed and because I am precious to you. If we come across a group of young men who concern me I will move quietly to the other side of you. I will do my best to make sure I do this subtly so that you do not notice— and so that they do not notice. If they concern me enough, I will pull my shoulders back and push my tits out. I will smile so hard at them they lose their eyesight. I will use this femaleness I have constructed as a barrier between you and the sharp, vicious consequences of being a different kind of man in this world.

We don't go to the dyke bar after dinner because we both know they won't serve me. They think they know who I am: that my heels and my seamed stockings signal that I am weak, and that my red lips and the flower in my hair make me less intelligent. And though you would be welcome there, you take me home with you instead. You take me home and we hardly say a word in the car. You and I are always talking to each other, whether we move our lips or not; my hand caressing your thigh at the stop light, your hand gently cupping the nape of my neck as we pull into your neighborhood.

Despite his enormous sacrifice my father could not protect me from the sharp, vicious consequences of being a working-class woman in this world. My body and my spirit carry the scars of rape and disease, and these are not things I would hide from you, even if I could. When we enter your house you slip your arms around my waist and pull me gently toward you. You close your eyes and you breathe me into you. Not just the gardenia and lavender and coconut: You breathe *all* of me into you. At the dyke bar they would have called me "pillow princess" and snickered, assuming it is my natural tendency to be lazy, mistaking the art of reception for sluggishness. I feel your breath on my neck and your cock hardening almost simultaneously and I know that we are about to have an amazing conversation. It is none of their business who fucks whom or who is on top or who grabs fistfuls of sheet and blanket in un-abandoned moments of merciful understanding. It is enough that we speak to each other this way. It is enough that you see and hear me for exactly who I am—even when who I am is something unnamable.

In my house my father got the biggest portions at every meal. This is not because he is a man and men get more. It is because he is a man who is beautiful to the women in his life. Behind closed doors we find many ways to feed each other, many ways to tell each other how beloved we are, and many ways to release the tension of living in their world beneath the weight of their assumptions. Behind closed doors we don't need to use their graceless words to make ourselves known. Decades later, at your house, you pull yourself away from me and tell me to wait for you. You return with a smile on your face and a bowl full of water. You reach up, pull the wilting flower from me and place it beside the bed. You weave your fingers through my hair and your eyes speak volumes of our history. You sit on your bed and ask me to come to you.

I walk slowly. I understand the way my short black dress hugs my body. I chose this dress specifically to delight you. I made myself smooth and soft to contrast the rough, abrasive streets you walk bravely through to get to me. We both know that I can eat chicken and put a sexist jerk in his place. As subtle as I think I am, we both know I would throw my body in front of a gang of bigots without hesitating for you. I want to feed you because you have constructed a masculinity that loves femme women. I know what they think I am, and I don't care because the closer I get to you the more I am certain that you know. Their words have no place here. What exists here is hunger, pure and driven. What exists is recognition. When you are not with me I want you to remember who you are and I want you to remember who your girl is and so I offer myself to your hungry mouth now. I give you all the words to all of the stories of my body and I read all the stories of yours. Before I sleep I will allow my ring-less fingers to drift softly over your belly just to make sure you are full.

This is how I love you.

On Living Well and Coming Free

Ryka Aoki

> *Living well is the best revenge.*
> —*George Herbert*

1.

Two years ago, I was in a self-defense competition. I'm a black belt, and this was a black belt contest, held in front of students and other instructors. Self defense competitions require that we demonstrate defenses against scenarios such as multiple attackers, broken bottles, knives, and so on. It's fun to see how other styles and arts deal with attacks, and when instructors are competing, there can quite a bit of showmanship and teaching mixed in with the actual competition. That day, all the other competitors were men, and they performed some wonderful techniques with finishing moves that ended in strangulation, broken bones, or a playful kick in the pants.

When it came to my turn, however, I thought of where and how a woman would be attacked. In the multiple attack scenario, I disabled my attackers—quick and hard, to ensure they would stay down—then stopped. But instead of a finishing flourish, I stepped back and reached for my cell phone.

I reminded the audience that when two men attack a woman, their objective is usually different from when they attack a man. I do not want a female student to risk additional harm by prolonging a street fight any longer than necessary. She should free herself, find a safe, public place, then call the police. Forget machismo—for a woman attacked, it is victory enough not to be killed.

The first requirement of living well is living.

2.

I never saw the point in idolizing conventional outlaws. If they were sublime or saintly enough, they got to ride off into the sunset like Clint Eastwood or Alan Ladd. Otherwise they all seemed to die young, either by execution or imprisonment, or in a blaze of glory.

But these outlaws never got a happy retirement, a nice pension, grandkids; you never see outlaws with grandkids. Not that I wanted to live like one of those pathetic farmers in a spaghetti western, but really, I don't want to rule out grandkids, either.

So: Let's demystify this whole outlaw thing, okay?

The outlaw as antihero has long been an American icon, though it's become less a working definition and more a desirable brand. However, for too many people, "outlaw" has come to mean confronting others with self-righteous, moralizing inflexibility. We justify ourselves as outlaws because we are *right* and the other side, whatever it may be, is evil, wrong, or stupid. In this situation, there can be no diplomacy, no discourse. The other side is demonized so thoroughly that any outcome short of obliterating the opposing viewpoint soils the purity of the cause.

Especially in times of uncertainty—war, economic downturn, or heck, breaking up with your first boyfriend—this circle-the-wagons-and-start-shooting mentality is an easy sell. It's Foucault meets Wal-Mart—no wonder everyone from Steve Jobs to Sarah Palin fancies him or herself a maverick, going rogue. Part of this is natural—in the face of danger, all of us will band in groups. It is safer to walk down a street together than alone. However, these groups themselves become a threat when in-group status becomes privileged, and there is a pressure to be part of a more and more conforming clique of "us," rather than dissenting and risk becoming one of "them."

Calls for gender studies symposiums and papers are rife with confrontational rhetoric and buzzwords that foster us/them discourse. We break gender, bust gender, punch gender in the mouth, and shove gender into a wood chipper. Shouldn't we know better than to use the same rhetoric as a college football coach? Declining to participate in the chest-pounding and vitriol is not a sign of weakness; it's a sign of disagreement. And disagreeing with someone else's definition should not mean that one is less savvy, less informed, or less committed to gender equality than someone who has just discovered Judith Butler. Or, for that matter, Judith Butler.

When one cannot be an outlaw without one's special outlaw hat, outlaw t-shirt, and outlaw reading list, then one needs to get a life, not another outlaw merit badge.

3.

There are other ways to look at being an outlaw. We're all outlaws at one time or another, simply because laws are designed to govern people as groups. No group of laws can encompass the varied desires and actions of an individual, and when any law omits or excludes us, we are by definition outlaw—not breakers of that law, but outside of it to begin with. We are all outlaws by omission.

When one cannot own property, nor vote, nor have access to education or bank accounts, one is by definition outside these laws. One cannot steal property if one cannot own property. In this sense, people of color, the poor, the differently abled, and women are outlaws by default. Sure, Jesse James was a famous outlaw because he robbed a train. But Rosa Parks was a far more relevant and effective outlaw because she rode a bus.

To live outside the law in this way is to understand that outlawry is not glamorous and rarely comes with a conference t-shirt. It's a debasing, life-threatening condition, in which the law doesn't consider you. Even during my martial arts demonstration, I realized that while most women would feel safe calling the police to report an assault, for trans women, dealing with the police is usually humiliating at best and dangerous at worst. It's more than prejudice; much of the legal system is simply not written to address trans people.

It does not seem to me, however, that shouting "Down with the police!" makes our lives better. It is tempting to hate police indiscriminately, but if two men have just attacked you with knives and you need to call the police—there had better fucking *be* police. It's more constructive to work with the police and help them begin to be more compassionate toward us. Members of the transgender community in Los Angeles and West Hollywood are doing brave, fierce, important work with their police departments to help them treat trans people with maybe a little more dignity.

To me, these are gender outlaws in the most nurturing sense of the word. No one is expecting miracles. But it's a start. If outlaws pursue the romanticized goal of erasing structures, both political and social, then we will have no shelters to subvert, reform, or protect us. The police, the women's shelter, and the hospital may be closed to many trans women, but as long as they are there, there is the possibility of change.

But should the structures be torn down, and gender mean nothing, then nothing will protect the weak from the strong.

Why can't we get beyond gender, you ask? Even with a third-degree black belt, a national championship, and decades of martial arts training, estrogen and age have made me physically weaker. Part of living in a gender binary is being able to say, Dude, you are not going to hit a woman, are you? I *want* a man to think twice before he hits me. I am not breaking the binary in this case; I am using the binary to get what I want.

Here's my Outlaw Reality Check—Is what we are doing helping individuals live well?

4.

Being a living trans person means vigilance. For a non-passing trans person, there is no safe space. It is not who we are kissing, but our very heights, our voices, and the size of our hands that catalyze hatred and violence. Forget activism; simply negotiating one's world every day, constantly judging, adjusting, scanning one's surroundings, and changing clothes to go from one role to another can be overwhelming.

Add to that cases of family disownment, poverty, homelessness, HIV. When a recent study of transgender youth reports that half their sample had entertained thoughts of suicide, and a quarter of them had made at least one attempt, I am not surprised.

How can we best help other genderqueer, trans, and gender variant people live better? Should we teach them to validate themselves by invalidating others, to focus their insecurity and anger on people who do not conform? Should we foster backbiting questions, like who is really trans and who is a poser? Should we teach them to police themselves and those around them to ensure that each is transgressing in the same way they are?

For me, the answer is clear. We can resist this temptation and declare that hurting should not beget hurt. A family, community, or village should tell its members that they can value their lives and their autonomy enough to say no—and should provide them the chance and even some guidance to find their own answers. Instead of questioning and invalidating other forms of expression and whispering that this person isn't "trans enough" or "queer enough" or "subversive enough," let us give people the support and affirmation that they may never have experienced.

In this way, being a gender outlaw can be much more than a brand name or a call to arms. It can be an opportunity to reflect upon and plan improvements to one's life. With so many obstacles and the constant threat of violence facing us, pursuing one's bliss is not a waste of time, nor a sign of weakness. It is living well.

It is the best revenge.

5.

As humans, we are rightfully horrified when we hear stories about victims of institutionalized genocide and persecution. The Statue of Liberty asks all other nations not for "your finest, your best," but "your tired, your poor." We demand marriage and reproductive rights and cannot understand why anyone would have the audacity to tell us who to love, how to live, or whose children we must bring to term. However, being aware of one group in crisis does not automatically mean one sees all injustice— and more importantly, it does not mean that simply because one detects no injustice, it is not there.

When a trans woman cannot be allowed in most women's shelters, this does not help her live better. When we deny services to trans women, especially crisis intervention services, we tacitly condone violence against them. We are saying either that a rape of a trans woman is not the same as the rape of a cis woman, or that a trans woman has lesser access to the term "woman" than a cis woman.

When the Irish immigrated to the U.S. during the potato famine, only idiots would have lectured them on Irish culture and its relationship with farming. Anyone with the slightest bit of empathy who saw these people would have seen that they needed food, not a theory that explained themselves to them. They were hungry. And in our community, where it seems that trans women get so little credit or consideration, rather than question how the penis or male socialization affects feminism or transfeminism, it would be nice to have some unconditional acceptance. And maybe gain some friends along the way.

6.

Ironically, even while trans women have been seen as lesser or ersatz females, their work has been treated precisely as women's work, with the same devaluation it has received since time immemorial. Just check out a history book: Women's work is scarcely even recorded, much less classified as historically significant, while every culture seems to have recorded its generals and dictators.

If I hear one more complaint about trans women not being activists, I am going to throw a fit. When people wonder why trans women still lip synch, or chase men, or worry about their makeup, instead of presenting papers and posting in newsgroups and holding meetings dedicated to busting up the binary, they commit the same misogynist crimes against women that men have been guilty of since the beginning of time:

"Why can't they act more like us?"

Trans women are doing their outlaw things, in their own ways, on their own terms. They are seeking entrance to institutions that have barred them. Why? Why did Rosa Parks ride in the front of the bus? Because she wanted to. Because it made her life better. Because she knew that was where she belonged. Instead of disregarding issues like old school drag and femme and passing and shoe size and body image as backward and ignorant, what about trying to understand that in these acts there is another type of narrative being constructed?

I think of my self-defense competition. Just because I don't bust a move to kill or injure my opponent does not mean I am a less accomplished martial artist. What it means is simply that my objectives and techniques are different.

Unless absolutely necessary, I will not fight to kill. I've never killed anyone, but I have hurt people badly, and I did not like the feeling. Not only do I dislike hurting people; I like living. I like the idea of someday meeting my grandkids. I refuse to fight crazy with anger. I find the patriarchy not guilty by reason of insanity. Besides which, it's not just the patriarchy: It's the crazy matriarchy, and the stepsisters and brothers and the twittering cousins and the whole nutty family that keeps threatening to disown you. I am not going to stop cooking rice porridge or hoping for a comfortable house with a garden simply because my batshit relative tells me it's not subversive enough.

7.

Living well is not an essay topic. It is not a theory. It is a practice. We must do it with intention, as often as we can.

For me, being an outlaw, being a class of person that the law does not address, means thinking beyond oppressed and oppressor. Outlaws are more than victims or charity recipients. Because we exist outside the laws, we shed light on the arbitrariness of these very laws. Accept that a trans woman is a woman and you have freed yourself once and for all from the dogma that to be female is to be a baby-making (or potential baby-making) machine. Accept that a trans woman is human and add another piece of evidence that we are more and other than the morphology of our bodies, our appearance, and our histories. In a society that preys on a woman's insecurity, *any* woman who feels beautiful inside and out is a gender outlaw. And when a trans woman can do this, despite the institutions closed to her, she should be celebrated, never scorned.

Being an outlaw means understanding that freedom is not a zero-sum game. Freedom depends on its abundance. For it to mean anything more than another layer of oppression, my emancipation necessitates the emancipation of others—even of those who have oppressed me.

8.

I took third place in the black belt self defense competition. Not too bad. Not for my first time back on a mat in years. I had been head judo instructor at UCLA and the coach of the Cornell judo team. But after I transitioned, I had nowhere to practice. My old dojo would not have me, and I was no longer in school. Over two decades of judo knowledge basically rotted inside of me for seven years. Because a group of queer martial artists had decided to form their own school, I finally was able to practice my art. Thanks to these gender outlaws and their positive, creative action, I finally had a place to be queer, to be a woman, to be trans, but most of all, to feel a mat under my feet and my belt around my waist. It felt like I was flying.

After the event, I changed in the women's dressing room.

And so ended seven years of searching, just to find a martial arts space where a trans woman could change her clothes undisturbed. I hadn't wanted a change in the rules, or special treatment, or special transgender classes and facilities. I just wanted to use the dressing room. And now, it was over. I wanted to dance and shout, "Look, motherfuckers! See? I'm not messing up your furniture!"

My hands were shaking as I shook my head and pulled out my pony-tail. My hair was a mess! After all that fighting, tufts of hair were kinked and knotted, tangled this way and that. I ran my brush through it, but it just made the knots worse. I knew the other participants were waiting for me to go to dinner, so I pulled harder. OUCH! I thought about pulling harder, or maybe cutting the tangles off with scissors, or a knife. . . .

Then I stopped. No one was telling me to rush. My new friends knew where I was and wouldn't mind waiting just a little while. I slowed down and remembered that the best way to remove tangles is to work the strands methodically, not from the top down, but from the bottom up.

It took a while, and there was some pain, but with patience, and a little faith, every tangle finally came free.

Faygele

Dane Kuttler

After the drag ball
with Faye Gala, the Jewish drag queen
who sang Sinatra,
you said I looked stiff
on the dance floor.

The glitter was falling
from your goatee like flakes
of girlstuff.

After I bit your lip,
you gasped

out of the dress
I need out

I tried to lift the straps,
but my hands were shaking.
Instead, your steadyhanded lover
unzipped you, while I
rubbed the hair on your shoulders,
pleaded through cuff links
and your old binder:

call me girl
I'm lost

You were naked like fish
returned to the ocean,
covered in sparkles
and bobby pins
calling me back,

girl, pretty girl,
I know you're under there,

I see you

I fucked you while wearing my father's tie,
and couldn't speak after.

the secret life of my wiener

cory schmanke parrish

What does my wiener do on the days i don't wear it? usually tame and mild mannered nestled in my fruit of the looms, does it long for the good life—open air and fields of wild flowers? on days when i believe it is tucked safe and snug in a bag of cornstarch in the top drawer of my dresser, does it carefully peel back the ziplock closure, hop down from the dresser, wave a quick hello to the dust bunnies under the bed and a gentlemanly how-do-you-do to the crumbs from last night's dinner in the kitchen, and merrily amble down the stairs to freedom? i hope it doesn't ride the subway, cuz man, new york is dirty and you know i don't wash that thing before i put it back in my pants. or does it stay home, content to frolick with its dearest love, my boyfriend's spare wiener? do they cuddle on the couch for hours, watching oprah and sipping tonic water? do they slap themselves together for a good time? or do they simply sit ball to ball, gazing into each others' fake pee holes? what is the secret life of my wiener? does it swing from the chandeliers, stretching to the floor and snapping back to shape? start gang wars with the silverware, forks down, spoons up? or stage elaborate competitions, racing my childhood slinky up and down the stairs? i may never know the secret life of my wiener. but if you see it one day, frolicking in the fresh-clipped blades of strawberry fields, could you please remind it to be home in time for dinner and to take a bath before bed?

In Our Skin

A.P. Andre and Luis Gutierrez-Mock

photos by Shilo McCabe

This essay is the transcript of a performance given by the authors at Trans As Fuck, an erotic performance-art showcase that takes place during San Francisco's annual National Queer Arts Festival. As mixed race, academic, pervy exhibitionists—as well as long-time friends and lovers—Luis and A.P. created a hot, intelligent piece examining the intersections of their mixed race heritages, (trans)gender identities, and desires for one another. In preparation for their ten-minute piece in Trans As Fuck, Luis and A.P. recorded a conversation about their relationship onto a CD. During their time on stage, performing for a crowd of 250 people, Luis and A.P. had sex with each other while the CD played. The audience responded with everything from dropped jaws to laughter to tears to intense arousal. The end result was an astoundingly intimate glimpse into Luis's and A.P.'s personal backgrounds, their struggle for visibility, and the sweetness of their relationship. Here is what was on the CD, and what the audience heard while watching the two:

Luis: Hey, welcome to In Our Skin, a piece by Luis Gutierrez-Mock

A.P.: and A.P. Andre.

L: I'm Luis, a queer, biracial, Chicano/white, transgender, FTM.

A: And I'm A.P. I'm a mixed, black/white, Jewish, bisexual, genderqueer femme who's sometimes a boy.

[Both laugh.]

A: We like having sex with each other, so we wanted to talk about that, and talk about our identities and what happens in the space when we're having sex.

L: A.P. and I have been having sex for a few years now. It's nice, seeing our relationship and our friendship really build off of us having sex, and having different types of relationships with each other. When we have sex, it's this special space that we create. I feel similarly when I'm having sex with other mixed-race queer folks, but with you and I, because we've been having sex for so long, it's very unique.

A: But one challenge has been negotiating the fact that we're both bottoms!

[Both laugh.]

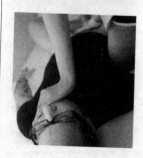

A: It's a lesson in figuring out how to take turns with each other. Because I don't think that topping is something that necessarily comes naturally, at least to me. But it's so much fun to watch you come that it inspires me to bring the top out of myself, in order to give you a good experience as a bottom.

L: When we first started having sex, it was in the context of you and I playing together while your partner was topping both of us. And then it turned into you topping me and I was your boy and doing service for you. And now it's moved on from there.

A: Yeah. So now there's a lot of turn-taking!

L: *[laughs]*

A: What I like about the space that opens up between us when we're having sex is that it's a place for me to play around with gender and also explore gender. I've been, over the past few years, trying to figure out what genders I am or might be and also figure out my personal relationship to black masculinity. That's been, at times, a scary process for me. So, when we're having sex and I'm able to use the space to play with the male parts of my identity and to play with being a boy, it feels very safe for me. I really appreciate that, because I feel like it's not a very safe world for the expression of black masculinity in any body. But in bed, in a sexual context with you and potentially with other people I might play with as a boy, I can go there with myself and see what it means to be masculine—well, I'm not a very masculine boy!—
[Both laugh.]

A: but see what it means to be a very femme-y boy, and have it be okay, have it be celebrated and eroticized. That's really exciting for me.

L: What I like most about our relationship is really being seen as all of my identities at once. That's something that I never have to worry about with you. It's something that I think about a lot, because I pass for white. And I'm starting to pass as a non-trans guy now. I feel like people perceive me as a white man, which is scary and doesn't reflect my identity or my history of growing up female in my very Mexican family. But when we're having sex, I feel really good in that space, and I feel like all of me is being seen. *[noticing the time]* Oh, we should make a little note.

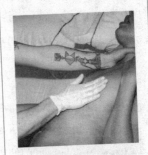

A: Yeah, we should switch now. Whoever is getting fucked should flip over.
[Both laugh.]

L: So, I feel like you see all of me. In learning what it is to be a Latino man, and to be a Latino man who passes as white, for me, it gets really intense. In good ways, a lot of times. But it's nice to be able to interact with someone sexually where it's not exotified in really fucking creepy ways, like where you're not asking me to translate things into Spanish for you. It feels really good. Just knowing that our identities, while they're really different, are also really similar—I think that's hot.

A: I agree.

L: I wonder what we're doing right on stage right now.

A: *[laughs]* Well, I think one of us is probably cumming right now. Or both.

L: *[laughs]* Yeah! That's another thing that I like. We both come really quickly and easily.

A: I think we have a similar sexual temperament. I have to say that you're probably the closest rival I've ever met, in terms of being really orgasmic, in the same way that I am. I haven't had sex with anyone else who can out-come me or come as often as I do. That adds to the playfulness, because we know what it's like to be on the other end and how to keep one another going. I think that's pretty hot, too!

L: I like it that sometimes when we're fucking, like, for example, when we were rehearsing earlier today, you were slapping me and punching me, and we were both cracking up in the middle of it—I like having that playfulness there as well.

A: In the past few years, as I've been exploring my gender identities, going beyond only identifying as femme, to, in some sexual spaces, identifying as a boy or playing as a boy, it's nice to have someone else there who gets it, and who can be a boy with me. We can just be, in some spaces, two boys together. Or we can top each other, but still be one playful boy topping another playful boy. That's pretty exciting, and it goes a long way towards me feeling comfortable exploring what it means to be genderqueer or what it means to be masculine in certain contexts.

L: While you've had a shift in your gender identity, I've had a shift in the type of people I date. I'm only dating people of color and mixed folks, which is really healing for me. At the same time, my attraction is shifting towards femmes and women, but you aren't either of those things in the context of our play. And even though my desire is changing, when we play together, it's still really sweet and really hot.

A: Well, I guess we're coming up on ten minutes. So, was there anything else you want to add, before our time is up on stage?

L: I hope people enjoyed the chance to see the space that we create when we're together. I know that we're enjoying it. We always do!

[Both laugh.]

A: That says it all! Thanks for having sex with me.

L: Thanks for, I'm sure, making me come a lot.

A: No problem. Any time.

L: Thanks to the audience for watching us have sex onstage, because that was really hot for us, too, I'm sure! [laughs]

A: Yeah, absolutely. Thanks, everyone!

Glitter, Glitter, on the Wall, Who's the Queerest of Them All?

Esmé Rodríguez (aka T. Kupin-Escobar)

I recently found a piece that I wrote to my drag mother, but never mailed, years ago:

> *If it had only been one hour sooner, or later, you might have missed me on that stage. You might have been drawn to someone else, a tube of lip-gloss, or a fresh cocktail. If the night had been other than a Sunday, or the evening rainy instead of crisp and dry, you would not have invited me to your home, taken my newness under your wing, and onto your lips. It was my second chance to have someone bring me into the world, a blank slate, washed clean of ethnicity, sex, gender, and antiquated regulations and ideals about love. "I Will Always Love You," was the song we danced to, me huddled in your elegant deluge, your long blonde wig cascading over my shoulder. One day later, it would not have been the song to which, when it plays, I must still lower my face, for fear of unearthing the abyss that you left within my soul.*

If it had only been March, instead of January, I would not still harbor that ridiculous photograph of the two of us, boa-clad, hand in hand, posed behind a life size picture frame, reminding me of the staunch box which you allowed to trap your heart. You insisted that you would be forever beside me. Now I find this remnant letter, applaud our time, and hope you are well, long and far away.

Drag incites, creates, and questions desire. It is an art that produces unseen vehicles and pathways upon which love, attraction, and stimulation travel. Staged and un-staged, I am a drag queen. When staged, I spend hours designing costumes, wigs, and make-up before my shows, and heavily padding my bras, hips, thighs, and buttocks. I have learned to walk, dance, and cartwheel in eight-inch platform heels in order to achieve the illusion, which is to be created through my character: the amplification of femininities and masculinities.

For ten years, I have been working as a queen. I am a permanent cast member in a variety of shows, and I produce and direct my own hybrid drag theater show. I have also toured national colleges and universities, speaking on Queer and Gender Theories in conjunction with live performance. This, after having been assigned "female" at birth, a label with which I do not self-identify.

My fellow performers often announce me to the stage by screeching, "And here's a chick with a dick who knows no boundaries!" ("Chick with a dick" being a common term of satiric endearment as queens bring each other to the stage for performances.) Some MTF trans friends, after scratching their heads in thought, have invented the label of "A Never-Op, Transsexual Male Cross Dresser" in order to loosely describe me. And while this certainly entertains my comedic senses, I realize that others often struggle as they attempt to articulate phenomena, or identities, for which language does not yet exist. Some people wonder how it is that I can be a drag queen, having been born without a penis. (I was a closet case for the first two years of my drag career, but was then outed as a non-male-born person.) I explain that being a drag queen is not always definable as "living as a gay man who wears a dress on stage." We, as queens, present, examine, question, incarnate, and reinvent the ideas of femininities and masculinities.

Drag performance is important politically and personally for me. It can function not only as an art, but also as an educational experience and a method of inquiry. In conjunction with formal gender theory and research, drag performance reveals even more innovative methods of expressing gender's multiple facets, especially the ones that we present in tandem. For me, being a drag queen is both an art and an identity in which I, along with colleagues and audiences, push past the fixed positions of binary gender roles and behaviors, in an effort to reconfigure antiquated notions of sex, gender identities, and politics.

The traditional medical community recognizes two opposite and exclusive sexes (those born outside of the specificities of medicine and biology are surgically or medicinally "corrected" to a sex chosen for convenience). I propose, since no two bodies are exactly the same, that the binary system is essentially flawed, and that there are innumerable types of "sexes." Just as gender is plural, so is biological sex. I reject the binary model of biological sex, and challenge that even the Natural Sciences are discourses. All existence and explanation is mere observance, interpretation, and translation of that which we believe to be fact.

Although I was labeled genetically female at birth, I have come to understand that personal identity is neither singular nor able to be represented within the categories which others attempt to put upon us. And since both gender and sex are multifaceted and fluid concepts, I reject the exclusive labels of "female" and "male." I welcome both male and female pronouns while *out of face* (drag slang for being out of drag persona) and prefer female pronouns when in costume.

Some of my identity markers are genderqueer, gender variant, trans, drag queen, boi, and gurl. While I have repeatedly considered transitioning from F to M, I feel that being perceived as male would not "cure" any of my gender variant thoughts or feelings. My gender identities do not fit into traditional binary categories. So, instead, I choose to navigate a kaleidoscope of uncharted territories, outside of the gender binary. I run from, make faces at, and stick out my tongue at "the gender police." And now and then, when they write me a ticket and I appear in court, I proudly declare myself "Guilty!" One hundred percent guilty of being a queer drag queen who unabashedly expresses herself.

Sometimes people ask me why it is that I identify with the label "boi" instead of "boy" or "man." The alternate spelling represents, for me, an intense and intentional rejection of patriarchy, and of other oppressive hierarchical institutions and social systems. That being said, "patriarchy" is not solely the function of male bodies, just as masculinity is an idea that may be embodied by any human form. Ideas are malleable. It is also true that I personally experience the potential in "boi" which supports a feminine strength, which aids in innovating and exists alongside other forms of masculinities. "Boi" is a label that queers the stability of patriarchy and the policing of bodies (lived genders). "Boi" questions the interpretations of masculinities and redirects theory, practice, and methodology.

Ironically, my gender identity is most stable when I am in drag and on stage. It is the staged presentation, embodiment, and innovation of the ideas of femininities and masculinities (which are concepts, not people). Just as in any community of people, there are a number of differences and commonalities between individuals. Paradoxically, I experience a grounded feeling in the transient and ephemeral nature of gender and performance.

Most people strive to find comfort in the stability of their identities. I am most comfortable wading amongst the instabilities and inconsistencies of my genders. When I leave my house for an evening out (*out of face*), I often pack a change of clothing, full-well knowing that I may not be comfortable presenting as one linear or traditional gender over the entire course of the night. I have walked out the door in a suit and tie and returned home in a full-length gown, or some stark combination of the two. Clothing choice is one of the many ways in which economically privileged people signal our gender expressions to others. That reason among others contributes to my vital need to examine and present the drag queen identity of my being, as drag constantly challenges the social connections between the material and the immaterial.

Gender and sex are manipulated by, and help to maintain, hierarchical systems of power and privilege. The more we intellectually interrogate oppressive systems, the better chance we have to promote optimistic changes toward equality and acceptance of all people, regardless of sex, gender identity, gender expression, sexual preference, race, class, ability, age, and religion. I believe that art, education, queer theater, and dialogue present themselves as positive and effective methodologies in this fight.

Having said that, I must recognize modern Gender Studies pioneers such as Kate Bornstein, Julia Serano, Gloria Anzaldúa, Judith Butler, José Esteban Muñoz, and many others. Through their scholarship and performance, they have courageously and thoughtfully introduced trans and queer identities to the majority public, outside of the traditional gay, lesbian, and bisexual boxes. Theirs was the task of demonstrating that trans identities do exist outside of traditional male and female categories. And it is from that point where I depart, proposing that just as trans has been introduced as another way of being outside the binary, that trans and genderqueer labels are limitless in the creation of individuals, expressions, and behaviors that they represent. There is no correct way, proper path, or universal experience required to assume or express a trans or queer identity.

I do not aspire to recreate or reconfigure bipolar ideologies regarding sex and gender, as that would be a futile reinvestment in antiquated forms of definition. Instead, I search for freedom of gender expression, gender identities, and social justice, and on the stage, I find it. On the stage, I find it, share it, and revel in it.

Transfag Robot Manifesto

Sam Orchard

transcension

Katie Diamond and Johnny Blazes

I HAD NEVER UNDERSTOOD ENGLISH GRAMMAR VERY WELL UNTIL I TOOK LATIN IN THE SEVENTH GRADE.

WHILE THE OTHER PRE-TEENS COMPLAINED ABOUT BEING FORCED TO STUDY A 'DEAD' LANGUAGE, I FOUND IT THRILLING.

ABLATIVE ACCUSATIVE NOMINATIVE DATIVE GENITIVE

THROUGH LEARNING CONJUGATIONS, I UNDERSTOOD HOW ENGLISH WAS STRUCTURED.

← preposition
← verb
← subject
→ object

•SUBFICTUMDICTUS•

→ word, language, speech

random word-ending the artist added

untrue, false, fake

under, underneath

accusative root

THE OTHER ENLIGHTENING THING ABOUT LATIN WAS THAT ONCE I HAD A HANDFUL OF VERBS AND A HEALTHY DOSE OF PREPOSITIONS MEMORIZED, I COULD FIGURE OUT THE MEANING OF ANY LONG ENGLISH WORD DERIVED FROM LATIN.

SO WHEN I ENCOUNTERED THE WORD TRANSGENDER AS AN ADULT, OF COURSE I IMMEDIATELY KNEW EXACTLY WHAT IT MEANT. **TRANS** IS THE LATIN PREPOSITION MEANING **ACROSS**, SO A TRANS-GENDER PERSON MUST BE SOMEONE WHO HAS CROSSED THE INVISIBLE LINE FROM ONE GENDER TO THE OTHER. SIMPLE: KNOWING LATIN HAD MADE THINGS SO.

①

BUT NOT
LONG AFTER,
I STARTED
TO REALIZE
THAT
THINGS
WERE NOT
AS SIMPLE
AS THEY
SEEMED.

THERE WERE PEOPLE WHO CALLED THEMSELVES TRANSGENDER WHO SEEMED TO FIT INTO NEITHER OF
THE PRE-EXISTING CATEGORIES OF MAN AND WOMAN.
AND FURTHERMORE, IT SEEMED AS IF I MIGHT BE ONE OF THOSE PEOPLE!

I CHANGED MY NAME, ASKED MY
FRIENDS, COLLEAGUES, AND
FAMILY TO CALL ME BY
GENDER-NEUTRAL PRONOUNS, AND
CONTINUED TO EXPRESS MYSELF
IN THE MULTIFARIOUSLY
GENDERED WAYS THAT I
ALWAYS HAD.

AND YET, I RESISTED JUMPING INTO
LABELING MYSELF AS TRANSGENDERED.

TRANS-GENDER:
across genders

BUT IF I DON'T BELIEVE THERE TO BE ONLY TWO GENDERS, HOW CAN I SAY THAT I'VE CROSSED SOMETHING? IF THERE IS NO HARD AND FAST LINE SEPARATING MASCULINE AND FEMININE, HOW CAN I HAVE CROSSED THE BORDER?

I EXPERIMENTED WITH CALLING MYSELF GENDERQUEER. DEFINITELY FIT. MY GENDER WAS AS QUEER AS ALL GET-OUT. BUT THERE WAS SOMETHING LACKING IN THAT TERM. OR RATHER, IT WAS NOT ENOUGH.

IF WE DIDN'T HAVE THESE LABELS: MAN, WOMAN, BLACK, WHITE, CHRISTIAN, JEW... COULDN'T WE ALL JUST BE PEOPLE? SO MANY WARS COULD BE AVOIDED IF PEOPLE WEREN'T SO OBSESSED WITH CATEGORIZING THEMSELVES INTO LITTLE FACTIONS.

WELL. YES. THEY CAN BE VERY DIVISIVE. IT'S TRUE...

SO WHY ARE YOU SO OBSESSED WITH FINDING A LABEL FOR YOURSELF?

I GUESS YOU'RE RIGHT ...

WHY DOES IT MATTER WHAT YOU CALL YOURSELF? AREN'T LABELS WHAT DIVIDE US?

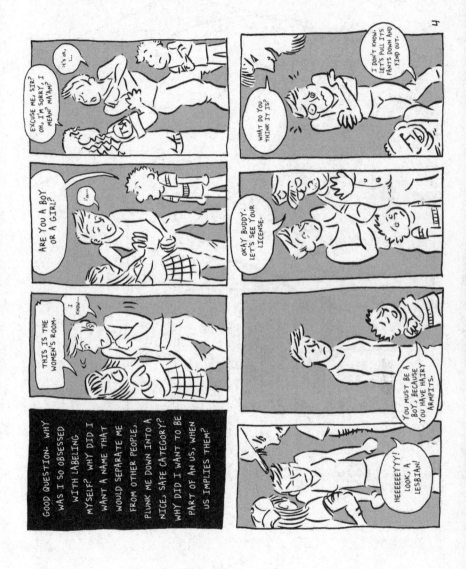

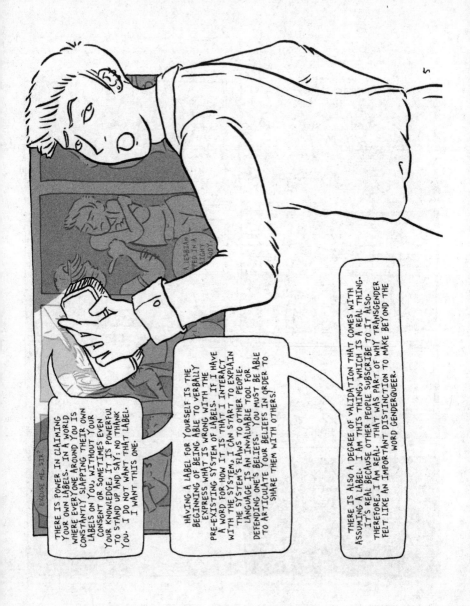

. . . which is why I'm as cute as I happen to be.

WHEN I TOLD MY BOSS I WANTED TO BE CALLED ZE AND HIR, AND THAT I WAS GENDERQUEER, SHE MISINTERPRETED THE TERM TO MEAN THAT I WAS DEFINING MY GENDER BASED ON MY SEXUALITY.

WHEN I WROTE HER A LETTER IDENTIFYING MYSELF AS TRANSGENDER, SHE UNDERSTOOD MUCH BETTER.

THERE WERE BOOKS FOR HER TO READ, ARTICLES, WEBSITES, REFERENCES. SHE HAD HEARD THE WORD BEFORE, AND THAT GAVE IT VALIDATION IN HER EYES, WHICH IN TURN VALIDATED ME.

BUT THIS IS DANGEROUS. RELYING ON OTHER PEOPLE FOR VALIDATION OF ONE'S EXISTENCE IS NOT A PRACTICE GROUNDED IN TRUE SELF-UNDERSTANDING OR SELF-ACCEPTANCE. I AM A REAL PERSON WITH A VALID IDENTITY BECAUSE I KNOW IT IS TRUE, NOT BECAUSE I BELONG TO A CLUB THAT OTHER PEOPLE SAY IS AN ACCEPTABLE WAY TO BE.

SO MY SEARCH FOR A LABEL, OR RATHER, MY SEARCH FOR A WAY TO FIT INTO THE EXISTING LABEL TRANSGENDER, DERIVED FROM ALL OF THESE: SELF-DEFENSE, ARTICULATION, RECLAMATION, VALIDATION. AND... A DESIRE TO BELONG. I DID NOT BELONG TO WOMAN OR MAN, AND WHILE I REJOICED IN THAT, SOME PART OF ME FELT HOMELESS. IT IS A VERY HUMAN DESIRE, THE DESIRE TO BELONG TO A GROUP.

BUT NOW I FOUND THAT I WAS NOT SO SURE I BELONGED TO THIS GROUP EITHER. AS A FEMALE-BODIED TRANSGENDER PERSON I PERCEIVED THAT THERE WERE CERTAIN STORIES TO WHICH I WAS EXPECTED TO RELATE.

I AM A MAN TRAPPED IN A FEMALE BODY.

I'VE ALWAYS KNOWN I WASN'T A GIRL.

I HAVE A CONSTANT SENSE OF SOMATIC DYSPHORIA.

I NEVER LIKED "GIRLY THINGS" WHEN I WAS A KID.

I FOUND MYSELF ASHAMED TO ADMIT THAT I HAD LOVED BALLET CLASS AS A KID--A KID WHO WAS QUITE CERTAIN I WAS A GIRL, WITH MY PETER PAN HAIRCUT AND THE FRILLY PINK TUTU THAT MADE ALL THE OTHER FIVE-YEAR-OLD GIRLS JEALOUS.

THERE SEEMS TO BE AN OBSESSION AMONG TRANSFOLKS WITH OUR OWN HISTORIES. WHY DO WE SIT AROUND TELLING THESE HAIR STORIES, BATHROOM STORIES, SCHOOL STORIES, FAMILY STORIES, STRANGER STORIES? ARE WE LOOKING FOR VALIDATION OF OUR PRESENT STATE IN THE STORIES OF OUR PAST?

AND THE MOST PERVASIVE OF THEM ALL:

I HAVE ALWAYS BEEN THIS WAY.

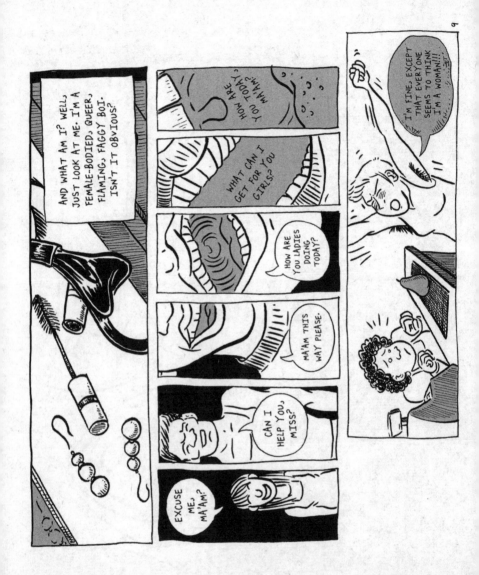

OKAY. I GET IT. I GET THAT THE HETEROSEXUAL HETERONORMATIVE STRANGERS I MEET MIGHT NOT PICK UP ON THE SUBTLE DIFFERENCES BETWEEN MY GENDER AND THEIR UNQUESTIONED, INGRAINED NOTION OF WOMAN. BUT... I DON'T SEEM TO BE PASSING IN THE TRANS COMMUNITY EITHER. I'M NOT PASSING AS TRANS.

I'M AFFORDED A LOT OF PRIVILEGE BY THIS NOT-PASSING. I'M NOT QUESTIONED IN RESTROOMS MUCH ANY MORE, AND NO ONE IS SURPRISED BY THE NAME OR GENDER ON MY DRIVER'S LICENSE. I AM IN LESS DANGER THAN MANY OF MY TRANS FRIENDS WHO ARE ATTEMPTING TO PASS AS CISGENDERED MEN, AND WHO MAY OR MAY NOT SUCCEED FROM MOMENT TO MOMENT. I'M NOT COMPLAINING ABOUT THAT PRIVILEGE, CERTAINLY. BUT THAT DOES NOT MEAN IT FEELS GOOD. BEING MIS-READ BOTH BY THE WORLD-AT-LARGE, AND BY ONE'S SUPPOSED PEERS IS SADDENING AND TIRING. I DO NOT FEEL THAT I FIT INTO MAN OR WOMAN, BUT IT SEEMS THAT I ALSO DO NOT FIT INTO TRANS.

NEITHER DO I.

I DON'T EITHER!

ME NEITHER!

I DON'T!

NOPE, ME NEITHER.

NOR I.

ME NEITHER.

~FIN~

Intermission

Kate Bornstein and S. Bear Bergman

Kate Bornstein: I still work that stupid koan, "The way you do anything is the way you do everything." I KNOW there's some cosmic resonance with all this breaking-the-binary-of-gender thing. That's what I'm searching for.

S. Bear Bergman: I hate that koan.

SBB: I hate it, because it's so true.

KB: Bingo. I hate it too, for the same frakking reason.

SBB: I am always looking for the loophole, and I can never find one, which I really resent.

KB: Oh grasshopper, we are the loophole.

SBB: 'splain, Zen Master?

KB: Before we went through our queer transformations, there were no loopholes to the culturally approved and mandated sex-and-gender binary system. Our bodies, our stories, our lives . . . there's never been anything like them. Sure, the way we did it was the way we did everything else in our outlaw lives. But the fact that we did it with sex and gender makes us the loophole that can now be used as a loophole in other binary systems of oppression.

SBB: And there's another thing all the pieces we selected have in common—they're both being and using the loophole. They're not in thrall of that system, and so they're not dependent on the rewards it offers for compliance.

KB: The NEXT next genderation is gonna talk about spirit the way this next gen is talking about sex.

SBB: But it is, in some places, a model of non-attachment. It turned out, for me anyway, that once I got free of most of the mandatory gender systems rewards for good behavior, I was able to kind of shop around for what rewards I did want, and from whom. Many of them, it must be said, were much tastier. Homemade. Sloppy, non-processed, improvisational, and really satisfying.

KB: ::applause::

SBB: Maybe that's part of why this Next Generation is able to withstand the slings and arrows not only of the macro-culture but also of some of their own/our own elders?

KB: ::the sound of one hand clapping wildly in appreciation::

SBB: ::laughing::

KB: It's the stupid, trite analogy of the willow that bends in the strong wind and never breaks. That's the queer throughline we're part of.

SBB: I don't want to set it up though like people who are green-haired gender resisters are somehow this advanced life-form, and those who see a comfortable place for themselves in the binary are just a little dull, or aren't brave enough. I worry about debunking one hierarchy and creating another.

SBB: I worry about a lot of things, but, you know . . . .

SBB: ::attempts to look bendy::

KB: ::jaw drops in amazement at your successful bendy look::

KB: That brings us to the argument about cis versus trans. And how you were accused of being cis-something. What was it exactly?

KB: Shortly after GO came out, I was roundly accused of not being an outlaw cuz I looked too much like a girl.

KB: Happy me.

KB: Old school me.

SBB: A cissexist. I was accused of being a cissexist and a trans-misogynist douche.

KB: Nooooooooooooooooo! See, you are not setting up the binary.

SBB: In any event. Do we have other things to say about the prefix cis-, or about language in general? I have usually come to these arguments with the idea that, basically, they're good. They're a sign of progress. That we as transthings now have the agency to have our own words and definitions of them, and insist upon them to linguistic passers-by, and that this represents a net gain.

KB: ::listening::

SBB: Except when the name-calling breaks out, I love when transpeople get excited or insistent about particular words. I don't enjoy the policing that sometimes goes along with it, but in a weird way I like that we feel it's *our* right to police them. That the language now belongs to us, and we can say how we're to be named. That's all, really.

KB: The same folks who crapped all over us about "tranny" compared me to Rush Limbaugh when I dared commend Neil Gaiman for writing a piece avoiding a politically correct POV on trannies, and writing us with warts and all. Bless Neil Gaiman's heart. He named his daughter after a tranny, Holly Woodlawn. And in his cosmology of The Endless, he made one of the seven above-the-gods characters a tranny . . . Desire, no less. But the same people who must have cis = bad, trans = good attacked Gaiman. And me.

KB: There's a new activism that's trying to grow up out of this slippery, queer identity of ours. No politics to date has ever been able to represent slippery with any articulate form of activism. So, they're digging their heels into anything that gives them traction . . . .

interlude

I am Tay, and my partner is Zan.

He is more gender fluid than I. I'm just a tranny girl, but I'm a chef in a mostly male environment, which keeps things interesting, and hot though not in the usually hopeful ways.

I'm forty-five and 'bout as transitioned as I wish to be. Zan is forty and a year into his meds, but really, let a dyke tell it, he never really was any sort of girl. He's much more fluid than I, as in, he paints my toenails when I'm asleep and I do not paint his. He is an academic and multilingual. I am a cook with a master's in writing who makes up stories and languages, but typically I remain in my female gender, even with a gruff voice and bawdy chef's 'tude. I quit smoking a year ago, and my lungs are hearty, but my voice remains more profane than profundo, basso or non.

We started this tranifesto about a year ago, and have been a-tweaking it ever since.

Short story: I was working in a grocery store in Dallas, Texas, where I landed after Hurricane Katrina, and I saw all these gaudily clad women, and I thought to myself, I'm transitioning gender just to become one of them? Holy shit, no fuckin' way! The rest, as they say, is h(er)story.

Here is our tranifesto. I love him and he loves me, and being trans is just icing on the cake, even if we're not very conventional or closeted about it. We both figure, if you're a hippy, and you're trans, its better to compost than to worry about what to wear.

—Taylor Thorne

It might not be a picnic, but there's a great buffet.

———

Part Four

The Manly Art of Pregnancy

j wallace

There are many ways to go about acquiring what they call "a beer belly." I chose pregnancy. Beer and wings probably would have been an easier route, but I've never been one for the easy route, and I embraced the manly art of pregnancy. I'm a short, stocky guy who over the last year has gone from chunky, to having a great big gut, and back to chunky again. Along the way, I've also made a baby.

Judging by the resources available, one might assume that pregnancy is distinctly a woman's affair. Books have titles like *The Pregnant Mom's Guide, The Working Women's Guide, The Prospective Mother,* and *The Hip Mama's Survival Guide.* Most of the books for men make it clear that not only is pregnancy for women, but the only men interested in pregnancy are heterosexual males: *What to Expect When Your Wife is Expecting* is typical. Even books which say *Dad's Pregnant* in large friendly letters on the cover turn out to be written for cisgender men in heterosexual relationships, and about how to deal with your partner's pregnancy in your relationship. Books for pregnant men are hard to find indeed.

If the La Leche League can encourage women everywhere to embrace *The Womanly Art of Breast Feeding,* I'm going to put in a plug for the Manly Art of Pregnancy. For those of you not yet familiar with pregnancy as a manly art, let me introduce it. The pregnant person is at once a biologist, a mechanic, a weight lifter, and someone providing for hir family. Women can do those things, of course, but our culture still views them as masculine things, and in this way pregnancy made me more of a man, not less of one. Before I was pregnant, I feared that pregnancy would make me into a woman or a lady. But it didn't; it made me more of a dude. I discovered that pregnancy is rife with things to worry about, and that after a while, gender stopped being one. Pregnancy became a manly act. Pregnancy helped me look, feel, and act more like an archetype of Man, and eventually lifted me to its pinnacle by making me a dad.

Let us begin with the aesthetics: Pregnancy is good for hair growth. Existing hair looks longer, darker, and thicker and new crops sprout up. I have new darker hairs on my chest, my leg hair is more visible, and even my beard is thicker. It's like taking testosterone all over again. Pregnant women often lament this, particularly when they are too pregnant to shave their own legs, but I loved it. The hair growth was so dramatic that I imagined pregnancy hormones being sold to people experiencing hair loss (because G-d knows they try to sell every other thing to people with hair loss). I imagined bald men rubbing Premarin on the tops of their heads, with bald Before, and hirsute After photographs.

When I took testosterone, not having a period was my favorite physical change. I loved the freedom it gave, the extra energy, not having to pay an extra tax for the femaleness I found miserable anyway. Pregnancy is the same. There is no bleeding. I can go about the world, safe in the knowledge that I will not have to beg a tampon from a co-worker. I no longer worry that a spare tampon will leap out of my bag at an inopportune moment. I don't worry that my period will stain my favorite date underpants. I skip the feminine hygiene aisle at the drug store entirely, and I am happier for it.

I recognize that these changes can be part of anyone's pregnancy, regardless of gender. The people that make maternity clothes clearly have thought about how masculinizing the physical changes of pregnancy can be and have therefore designed maternity clothes to re-assert femininity. Why else would they invest so much time and attention in making maternity clothes so very feminine? Seriously. Maternity clothes are pink, pastel, or floral, or all of the above, with liberal use of lace, bows, and ribbon. Maternity clothes flaunt curves, and they *flow*. It's very hard to look serious in most maternity clothes. In addition to all that, many of them make you look like you are four. When I first told my boss that I was pregnant she was very clear with me that if I showed up to work in maternity clothes, she would send me home to change. I can assure you that she meant it in good humor, but her point was well taken. So, I figured out what paternity clothes look like. As it happens, you can get through much of a pregnancy in larger shirts, larger jeans with suspenders, chef pants, and overalls. If the clothes make the man, the masculine art of pregnancy ignores the rack of maternity clothes. The secret advantage to this is that without the maternity clothes, no-one knows you are pregnant. You can walk around hiding a whole tiny person in your abdomen. Never once did a stranger put hir hand on my belly, gush about how I was glowing and ask how far along I was. The masculine art of pregnancy retains at least a little privacy.

Of course the challenge to this was changes in my chest. Pregnancy makes your chest grow. Before being pregnant I was a happy binder-wearing guy, smoothing my lycra undershirt down over my boxer briefs, but rapid growth in the chest department necessitated the first-trimester purchase of chest restraining devices. I put it off as long as I could. I tried shopping for things on my own, discreetly, like a shy straight guy shopping for a new girlfriend—but apparently these things are sized, and it's not like they encourage the "shy straight guy" to go into the change room and try things on. It became clear that I would need to be fitted, and I eventually resigned myself to this. I chose a local shop where I heard they had good fitters, walked up to the counter and asked in a manly, clear voice for assistance fitting me with maternity/nursing bras. Manly pregnant people ask for help with perfect confidence that they are entitled to good assistance, and I found I got good assistance in return.

And then there's this—I grew a penis. Transition-wise I've never really wanted to have genital surgery. Sure, there have been times, in beds and in kayaks, when a penis would have been handy, but for me it's not worth actually having one surgically attached. That said, at our twenty-week ultrasound they showed me grainy black and white pictures of a tiny penis I'm growing. I know not all pregnancies go this way, and it's not as if I decided to grow a penis rather than a vagina, but here I am, growing a penis. Had I known that exposure to sperm would awaken this ability in my body I might have spent more time in bathhouses and other seedy locations, but never mind, I can now add it to the list of things my body can do.

Pregnancy does mean making some life changes. I developed the art of seeming chivalrous while not lifting over forty pounds. I came to understand that sometimes, being manly is about knowing what tool to use. At seven months pregnant, the right tools to use to get a seized tire off one's car are a cell phone and roadside assistance. Crawling under one's car to strike at the tire with a hammer is not manly; protecting one's family and using a cell phone is. "Protecting one's family" is a manly pregnancy mantra. When the signs on the outside of a building warn that there has been an outbreak of fifth disease and pregnant people should not enter the building—you obey them, you do not enter, even when it means recruiting a nice lady to go inside and explain that you are not coming. Even when she goes inside and says "There is some guy, outside, who says he cannot come in because he is pregnant. . . . "

Pregnancy does not mean you lose access to your usual manly haunts, like the barber shop, and your local auto mechanic's. Even with the kid's kicks visible under the barber's towel, my barber did not notice my manly pregnant condition. We had the same conversation, and he gave me the same haircut and straight razor shave that he always does—and I gave him the same tip. The auto mechanics still called me sir and talked to me as if I know what the various engine parts are all supposed to do. It appears that if you're a guy, pregnancy does not make you a woman: it just makes you fat.

It's also easier to think about pregnancy as a manly activity if we butch up the language we use. I trained midwives, a doula, Ob/Gyns, and even a lactation consultant to talk about "pregnant people" not "pregnant women," or "pregnant ladies." A number of ciswomen friends had also complained that when they became pregnant they went from being "women" to "ladies" and they found the prissiness of the word uncomfortable. They too found "pregnant person" a better fit, especially if it meant not being referred to as a "lady" all the time. If we talk about "nursing," focusing on the action of providing for one's child rather than "breastfeeding," focusing on a body part assumed to be feminine, even this activity can sound more manly.

Pregnancy made me a dad. Pregnancy has been making dads out of men since about nine months after sex was discovered. I know fine men who have become dads in a variety of ways, some by love, some by adoption and fostering, some by other means, and I do not believe that there is any one traditional way of going about it. There are more common and less common ways, but all of them have a history and tradition. I became a dad through pregnancy and birth. Along the way, people who love me created the language of "bearing father" and "seahorse papa." We're queers, and we are well versed in creating the language we need to describe our realities. We will bring our world into being through words, as we bring babies into being through our bodies.

In the end, I gave birth to my son via a caesarean section. I have a small neat scar on my abdomen that I think of as "the baby escape hatch." Scars are manly. As I was recovering, I realized that the next time some intrusive person discovers I am trans and asks me if I have "had the surgery," I can say "yes" and go on to describe my c-section. They never say what surgery they mean, and a c-section is generally recognized as a gendered surgery.

In the hospital, after the birth, I was snuggled up in bed in my pajamas, holding my small son, when the public health nurse strolled in. She looked at me in the hospital bed, at the baby in my arms, and around the room. Then she looked again, and clearly did not find what she was looking for. "Where's the mom?" she asked. The simple answer is that there is no mom. Children need love and support from a parent, not a gender. Parents, not necessarily moms and dads, raise children, whether they are boys or girls. The public health nurse stammered an apology, and fled. I've been rehearsing better answers to that question since—better answers that say his family is not your business, keep your assumptions to yourself.

I've become a dad changing diapers, holding a baby, reading books to someone who can't really focus his eyes yet, a dad who was up many times last night with the baby and who is now blurry-eyed from lack of sleep. I do dadly things, including many things other dads do, and things I remember my dad doing. I'm also a dad who nurses, who gets up in the night to feed the baby without having to heat bottles, which I understand is an uncommon dad kind of thing to do. But I do it for my small person. I want the best for my child, which I understand is a common desire of good dads.

I'm a dad you might run into in the library reading to my small child, a dad in the park carrying my baby on my front, explaining the world to him, a dad who plans to teach my child to love insects and look at ants and caterpillars, a dad who'll head off in a canoe with his small person. I look forward to being the dad helping my child bake cupcakes and discover the joy of gardening, and celebrating his artwork. When you see me, what you see, and who or what you think I am has been totally eclipsed by the dad my small person sees, knows, and loves. I'm his dad, and in the tiny world of our family, that is what really matters.

Transgressing Gender at Passover with Jesus!

Peterson Toscano

Excerpt from *Transfigurations—Transgressing Gender in the Bible*

I once met someone special, one who some would say didn't quite fit. It was about the time of the Passover. Jesus didn't tell us where we would celebrate the Passover; he often kept his plans secret to the last minute. We began getting word from our families inviting us to spend the Passover with them. They added, "You can even bring the teacher, although he does smell funny."

It was the day before the Passover when Simon Peter persuaded me to ask Jesus, "Rabbi, where will we celebrate the Passover?"

Jesus replied, "Perfect. I want you, Thomas, and Philip to go into the city. There you will find a man carrying a pitcher of water. Follow that one home and say to the master of the house that we have need of a place for our Passover. There you will find an upper room fully furnished. Go make preparations there."

Simon Peter exploded. "Teacher, this is outrageous! There are no empty rooms in Jerusalem. We needed to make plans weeks, months ago. Besides, you send them on a fool's errand, to find a man carrying a pitcher of water! Everyone knows *only* women and children carry water! They will be walking around the city for days."

But Jesus said, "Go; you will find it just as I tell you."

So Thomas, Philip, and I got up and approached the city gates. We entered and turned towards the wells. And sure enough, in the distance, we saw someone that appeared to be a man carrying a pitcher of water. Well, the story behind this one!

Earlier that day Levi had gathered all his family at his father's house: his parents, grandparents, aunts and uncles, cousins, brothers and sisters, and all of their children.

He said, "Dear ones, we are about to commemorate the Passover, our deliverance from bondage into new life, and I confess that for much of my life I have felt like a slave. Oh, not that you treated me badly! It's just that . . . you remember when I was little, I used to play with my sisters and my girl cousins. You said, 'It's just a phase. He'll grow out of it,' but I never did. I just grew secretive. Through the years I realized that there was something wrong with me. The outside of me didn't match the inside. Inside I always felt like a girl growing into a woman, but outside you only ever knew me as Levi. So I turned to God and cried out to the Lord, God who desires truth in the inmost part, and God has given me peace. So in honor of the Passover, I want to begin to live my life outwardly as it has always been inwardly, as female, and from now on I want you to call me Miriam."

It was as if a demon had materialized in front of them. There was ranting and raving, yelling and wailing. Rending garments in mourning. Mothers dragged their small children out of the room, while the father raged around the house, "Look what you're doing to your mother! You're ruining Passover!"

Miriam stood, still, in the midst of the chaos. Then she saw it, the empty pitcher. She reached for it. Her father grabbed her hand, "*Young man*, what do you think you're doing!"

"Father, I am a woman, I want to help with the preparations for the Passover."

"*Young man*," her father said, "if you leave this house with that pitcher, no good will come of it!"

"Father, you know I have always honored you and mother. Come good or evil I do not know, but one thing I do know. I must obey God."

And for the first time since she was little, Miriam picked up the pitcher and walked out of the house. The neighbors looked on in shock and horror that someone from such a good family would be doing something so outrageous. Miriam continued to walk through the streets holding the pitcher.

She approached the well. The other women laughed at her as they moved out of the way. There at that well she plunged that old clay jar into the cool, cool waters and placed it onto her strong, strong shoulder and turned to go home.

It was about then that we saw someone who appeared to be a man carrying a pitcher of water. We ran up to this one and Philip said, "It is just like the teacher told us!" Thomas asked, "So is it true that you have an empty room where we can have our Passover?"

"Oh, yes, thanks to me, all the rooms are now empty."

Then I asked, "Would you like me to take that from you? You must feel awfully embarrassed holding it."

"Oh, no, it feels very comfortable, just right. You see, I am Miriam."

Today's New Name May Be Tomorrow's Old

Sassafras Lowrey

I was prepared to become an outlaw when I went on testosterone. I wasn't prepared to be an outlaw when I went off it. When you see me now, I look like a girl. When you see me, you won't believe this is my story. If you look past the tattoos, you'll think I look like a respectable woman in her mid-twenties. I don't look trans. I don't look like I spent years with sideburns. My long hair makes you think gender has never been a struggle for me. It makes you sure it isn't now. When you look at my made-up face, you don't know that I shave every morning, the permanent effects of transgression. Gender has always been my addiction and my obsession. It's defined my art and life. Gender has always been my most cherished playground.

I didn't learn about gender in any book. I didn't learn gender in a Gender Studies classroom. I learned gender on the streets, in youth centers, and in the self-created genderfucking queer gutterpunk families I joined when no one else wanted me. In my world gender was something to be done, not studied. It was something to explore with no limits: a free-fall towards fabulous.

My transgression wasn't encouraged or celebrated. I lost my home and parents. My friends were beat up in the streets and we all knew better than to call the cops. I was pushed out of neighborhoods, moving every other month because the neighbors didn't like not being able to tell the gender of the string of lovers who came through my door. No one could find jobs, regardless of how "protected" we were by the city's non-discrimination ordinances. The stores and restaurants never said it was our gender that made us unemployable; it was our hair, our piercings, our tattoos—we just weren't the right "fit," but I knew it was because I didn't check "male" or "female" on the application.

We made ourselves real. We created genders that we had never seen and scholars had never written about. We broke rules. We made bodies ER doctors didn't understand, never finding quite what they expected when we reluctantly shed our dirty workpants onto the sterile examination room floor.

I was fighting for survival. I was struggling to understand my history. I spent my days comparing scars with kids who wore as many as my own, but at night I was alone with no option but to try to make sense of the body I had. There were nights that stretched past morning, but I knew if I could make it to sunrise, on the wall of the youth center would be hanging a white board that said:

Old name	New Name	Pronoun

Everyone knew to check it every day, because in our world, today's new name could be tomorrow's old news.

I stopped being my mother's little girl at seventeen. I became a boy the first time I sucked cock. I felt the possibility of created gender. My first cock was bright purple and "novelty," the only way they could legally be sold. My boifriend took me to get my first binder, a thick bandage like a back brace that got tighter throughout the day. On my knees, before his cock, he called me his sweet boy.

I ran from destiny and expectation into those molding Portland basements and living rooms crowded with bike parts. As an only child who'd always longed for siblings, I found a brotherhood. I became a man. I seduced other trans men in the kitchens of punk houses and at shows. We were a gang of tranny fags, running wild through the wet streets. We found genesis. We made new worlds. Building bodies and galaxies out of dust, vegan cookies, and nicotine.

Languages formed out of lives so big that English could never explain us. We joined alliances, waging wars against our own flesh. Our bodies the battle fields. Together we sent up white flags of surrender, finding momentary peace. Redrew the maps, felt the topography shifting beneath each other's touch. Wispy sideburns, the way a lover's hand felt against bound-down chest was all we needed to prove to ourselves we were real. We were doing the impossible, changing in ways our parents never imagined. We were giving birth to our own lives, naming ourselves out of baby books or rebirthing ourselves with names that came to us, soaked and cold from a Portland rainstorm. Wet and dirty, I crawled into my bed, cradling the memory of birth.

I remember the first time I sank needle into flesh. The rush of power, of creation. I was terrified and turned on. This was performance art. My body the only prop I needed, the streets and punk houses of Portland my stage. North Portland still haunts me. Killingsworth to Lombard, I walked those streets cloaked in darkness, a soundtrack of riot grrrl and folk recorded in Alberta basement studios. Making stages from propped up pallets, learning to silkscreen with weak Oregon sunshine, and stealing double-sided copies. On the edge of genesis I created, loved, and fucked,

as bodies shifted and savings accounts ebbed and flowed with the seasons. Surgery funds traded for rent, dinner out when food stamps were low. Art was everywhere. Walls and skin covered with layer upon layer of color, image, and meaning bleeding together. My cuticles crusted with spray-paint, glue, copy-toner, and cum.

My transitions have never been fixed, but I told the therapist they would be. My gender outlaw family taught me about survival, how to pass when we had to and celebrate when we didn't. I told lies to the therapist to get what I needed. I told him I'd always felt like a man. I told him about pretending I was a boy when I was five, and I left with my letter, rode the bus up winding Portland hills to the pharmacy, and that night pushed liquid masculinity into my thigh.

I didn't tell the therapist my favorite childhood game was called "sex change," inspired by fleeting talk show images before my mother flipped the channel. I refrained from sharing that the point was to blur the boundaries. Teal washcloth swiped from the mildew-encrusted bathroom, rolled tight into the crotch of my pink crossword puzzle patterned panties. Carefully stroking the bulge visibly peeking out from under my belly, the tight bright spandex of my leggings pulled tight across it.

I had to quit the Future Farmers of America or risk being kicked out for refusing to wear a skirt. That was another good story I told my therapist. I never told him I grew up praying to feel safe enough to be beautiful.

When I came out as femme, I committed suicide. I killed off the boy I'd been trying to be since elementary school, when I made collages out of the baseball cards I wished I could find joy in collecting and families of my toy cars, rolling them from room to room of the doll house I claimed to hate. Claiming femininity meant facing a fear I'd held since childhood of being seen as vulnerable and weak. When I came out as femme, I assassinated the man I'd struggled to become with hormones. I killed off what wasn't working and began to play with gender in new directions. As a small child performing sexual reassignment surgery day after day in the secrecy of my bedroom, I steered clear of femininity. It was too dangerous, until seventh grade when my mother and stepfather separated for a year and femininity became safer. I became a drag queen. I strode through the carpeted halls of my junior high in platform traffic cone orange pumps, argyle tights and fluorescent dresses. I wore costume earrings, painted my nails each morning to match my outfit. I'd skipped direct to womanhood. Though I lacked the words, I knew gender was about performance. My pre-teen foray into femininity lasted six months of that school year, and when my step-dad came home in the spring I returned to jeans and sweatshirts and was the only girl at co-ed baseball tryouts.

My journey towards femme began with being claiming the identity of a bearded lady. I grew out my bi-hawks and beard, bought a pushup bra. I started wearing pin-up dresses and heels; I never shaved my legs. Drunk men on Vaseline Alley would ask me if I "bought those titties in San Francisco" and teenagers would snap pictures of me with cell phones before running away laughing. I felt powerful. The year of the circus, as I like to call it, was the most visible my gender has ever been. It was a time of self-reflection and outward presentation, but more than anything it was about proving to myself that femininity was just one more way to fuck with gender.

A year later, I quit testosterone for the final time. I learned femme from the best. During my years as a boy, I was watching and learning from the fiercest femmes, the ones who did this while the rest of us were shaving our heads. I learned to do femme from the riot grrrls who rocked the rugby socks off of andro dykes, and I learned femme from southern rebel princesses who could fuck, fight, and change the oil in the car without messing up their manicures. The first and best femme I studied was the ex-wife of an ex. I never had the nerve to look directly at her because she made her (understandable) hatred of me no secret. My eyes peering out from under a baseball cap would rest on the edge of her hip, the blade of her collarbone. Behind her eyeliner was a glare sharper than any knife. She wore Wal-mart lipstick and left traces of it on bois' shirt collars, intentionally. She taught me femme armor.

Femme has been just one more stopping point on the gender transition that has come to define my life. I am not a woman, although I pass for one. I don't "look trans." Growing up, I was never a girl. As a teen, I rebelled against expectation. This is not a de-transition or regression. Femininity is new territory for me.

Calling for the recognition of self-love as a legitimate relationship in the game of life

Andrea Jenkins

Who We Are

Transwomen and transmen, streetwalkers and hookers,
we direct city planning, drive your buses and fly your planes,
we are librarians, attorneys who fight for our rights,
creators of movements (remember Sylvia Rivera at Stonewall), we are professors, but most of all we're human, we
are the Leslie Feinbergs, the Susan Kimberlys, the Renee
Richards and Brandon Teenas, the Black and Latino children
dying in the streets because our mamas are too embarrassed to let us come home. We are all around you but
sometimes you don't even know it.

What We Do

Challenge all of your preconceived notions of the false
binary theory of gender, do drag on your stages, take the
heat along with all others who might be men that are super-
effeminate or women who are hyper-masculine, we seek
out safe bathrooms and friendly faces in a crowd 'cause it's
nice when you get a smile, we fight for the "girls" locked up
in men's prisons and the "boys" locked up in the women's
prison and write words, beautiful words.

Why We Pray

Because gender discrimination is a form of lawful
discrimination, because we can be fired from our
jobs or evicted from our apartments just for being
ourselves, because the American Psychiatric Association
still labels us as mentally ill, because too many transsexuals
die every day at the hands of murderers that hate
themselves and take it out on us.

The Resolution

Whereas, many men and women for that matter
have just walked on by, and

Whereas, the oceans that bound this part of the world
are not big enough to contain the tears that have been
shed many nights on end, and

Whereas, the only tragedy one suffers is the failure to
recognize the virtues in one's own identity, and

Whereas, torture can be defined as doing the same goddamn
thing over and over expecting different results, and

Whereas, the malady plaguing the human condition
is a lack of self respect, and

Whereas, dictators prey on lonely souls and condemn
them to a prison of self-destruction, and

Whereas, "we may never pass this way again," and

Whereas, just to be clear this is not a fucking love poem, and

Whereas, if it were though it would be about loving
your neighbor as you love yourself, problem is
most people can't stand themselves:

Therefore Be It Resolved, that I will manifest the love and
abundance in the universe and hold it dear in the darkest hour
of the night, and stroke every inch of my beautiful body for the
sheer joy of it (and for good measure) and

Be It Further Resolved, that I will not give a shit what anyone
else thinks that I take myself to a movie and a classy dinner,
nor will I seek the affections of those who refuse to respect the
intensity in which I share this bounty, and as a matter of fact,

Be It Much Further Fucking Resolved, that self-love is indeed the
only relationship that really matters and anybody that tries to
tell you different don't know shit about love.

Why You Don't Have To Choose A White Boy Name To Be A Man In This World

Kenji Tokawa

The bar was loud that night, I will admit that much.

I had, as usual, been carded on my first order and was sipping my Stella way too fast when my friend turned around from the conversation she had been having to introduce me to her conversee.

Kenji, this is Kristen.

Kristen had one arm extended and squinted at me through a smile.

Sorry, didn't catch your name.

Kenji. My name is Kenji. Good to meet you.

As if the act of knowing my name confirmed the appropriateness of finally grasping my hand in a clammy handshake, Kristen took it—and then blew it.

Candy? Yeah, nice to meet you too.

Wow, that's a new one! Here we go.

No. Actually, it's Kenji. My name is Kenji.

Oh I'm sorry. Kenji. . . .

That wasn't so bad.

. . . .like Benji, right? Benji the dog!

Dog! O Hell no! Who does this person think. . . .

. . . .Can I call you Benji?

Jaw clench. Air chest fill. Spine rigid snap. Handshake over. My friend watched in horror as I dropped my voice to a register that is in fact more like a growl and proceeded to close down Kristen's unfortunate and (probably unconsciously) racist sense of humor.

"No.

Not like Benji.

Or a dog.

It's Kenji

and it's Japanese.

Just like me."

Kristen probably smiled and then found a reason to disappear politely. Some by-standers sent me congratulatory hand gestures as I went to look for the bathroom. My friend, she got over it.

In this situation, "Adam" would have done much better. I know that "Brandon," "Cayden," or anything Celtic would also have been easier names for our dear Kristen to shake hands with. But the fact of the matter is that, although I have a quarter Celtic blood sharing my veins with my biweekly testosterone shot, my white mother gave me a Japanese name and in this tradition, I renamed myself with another Japanese name. The other fact of another matter is that for me, being trans does not mean I have to dismiss my Japaneseness.

(Not so) Androgynous "Ethnic" Names

I am one of those half-white mixies that on Turtle Island (aka North America, as the colonizers brought it) never ever ever passes as white. A few times, folks guess Japanese, but lately it's been Filipino—like twenty-first century FTM spokesman, Thomas Beatie. And that is beautiful, don't get me wrong. I'm flattered to be mistaken. But usually, except in the case of Kristen, my name gives me away as both Japanese and male. People tend to have heard of a male character named Kenji on certain Capcom video games in which I am an ass-kicking ninja. And all of this works according to my plan.

I was raised with a very common, very flowery, feminine Japanese name. My mother, bless her, didn't actually know the meaning of the name that she fell in love with in a Japanese fairy tale (translated to English) she read while pregnant with me. So my parents asked my Ogichan about it. Joy and beauty, he said, and that was that. Lucky for them I came out a girl. Well, maybe not so lucky now, ha.

In Ontario, where I grew up, there are not many Japanese-Canadians. Going to an Italian Catholic school didn't give me much reference for understanding how gendered my mother's favorite name was. In a highly Latinized linguistic environment, ending with a 'ko' is perhaps a lucky trait in a name for a tomboy. However, for a young transman with any sense of the Japanese from which his name came, it is *verybadneedtochange*. By the time I got to university, I was meeting more and more people who knew other girls and women with my name. Slowly, the 'ko' was transforming for me: It wasn't as masculine as the thought I had been hiding behind all these years. It was definitely a girl's name. That not-so-androgynous 'ethnic' name of mine became something I needed to move away from.

Choose a white one, it's luckier

In the fall of 2008 a colleague of mine, Diego Macias, and I presented a workshop at a trans conference in Peterborough, Ontario. Our workshop revolved around some issues trans masculinities of color are dealing with in the face of white-centric patriarchy. Preparing for the workshop, Diego and I found ourselves fixated on fixation: the fixation masculine self-identified folks of color have with white names. We noticed that Celtic seems to be really hot right now in the renaming of masculine-identified folks. The fad has become a priority in the renaming process, even for people of color. This is not to say people of color can't have Celtic names; often, though, a person whose former name was a name from their own culture will change to a Celtic or other anglocentric name in choosing a new masculine signifier.

We talked about how this culture of white supremacy presents the white male body as what is normal for masculinity. Along with the body comes the acceptable set of names. Along with a presumed whiteness comes respect. Along with this respect comes confidence and safety to move about in this world as masculine self-identified. The education system and other big institutions of influence in our lives rarely encourage us to pay any attention to our cultures of color and our family histories in a proud way. Thus many folks of color find ourselves in the same boat with white folks, not knowing the proper use of many 'ethnic' names, how they are gendered, or what significance they hold.

This racialized gendering of names gets in the way for people who need to make their gender obvious in the dominant culture. Like my name before. Ending in "o" made my name seem masculine in this culture, while in Japanese culture the name is very feminine. Ending in "I" makes my new name seem feminine in English, while in Japanese it is very much a boy's name. Passing becomes more difficult with a name that doesn't immediately communicate gender to people from English, French, Italian, Spanish, or other backgrounds of colonial power and dominance. At least with a familiar name like Adam, even if they clock you on sight, they have to do a double-take before finalizing how they perceive your gender. In a culture still under colonial rule, with a name like Akira and not enough money for hormones or surgery . . . good luck, Japanese trans boy, good luck.

Combine the rewards of adopting a more white form of masculinity with the absence of racial self-exploration and the embarrassment of having your gender mistaken, and we have a situation ripe for creating a bunch of men and boys of color with chosen white names. For instance, Thomas Beatie, Oprah's first pregnant trans man, is mixed-race, much like myself. He too has a white mama, an Asian daddy, and originally, an Asian (Filipino, influenced by Spanish colonization) surname. The benefits of taking it whitely are obvious.

Know your history, make history

Perhaps most difficult, for me, is that so often trans folks of color are told they are "doing a white thing" by being trans. As if the gender binaries of male and female were universal, and universally adhered to, in every culture. Absolutely not so: There is a rich history of third gender or otherwise non-male and non-female specific people in many cultures, including the pre-Spanish Philippines. In the islands known now as the Phillipines, *binabae* were high order religious authorities of mixed-gender, just as gender-transforming deity Kuan-yin is still highly esteemed in Buddhist tradition today. The only article that stuck with me from my first year women's studies class pointed to 17th-century Chinese reports of people who were born male and ended up female or vice versa. These Asian gender-crossers were considered to be examples of the fluid nature of yin and yang, not perverse or worthy of ridicule as many people of gender-transitioning experience are considered today. In many cultures of color, pre-colonial history shows societies valuing these people specifically because they are outside the norm of gender, often choosing them for positions of spiritual power and authority. However, witch hunts and other rigid reforms in gender occurring in the white west, coupled with the need to topple indigenous authority figures, influenced European colonizers to seek out and destroy these ambiguously-gendered people. Transphobia is now rampant in formerly colonized places, as a legacy of colonialism. Violent and strategic colonization means that history validating Thomas's and my trans experience as Asian genderfuckers is hard to come by.

And now, because of this erased history, it is our very Asianness that is often used against us to make transphobic and racist comments: "Oh, it must be hard with your Baachan, more so than on your mom's side," or "Hey, we don't do that kind of freaky shit, we're Asian." Non-Asian people of color can relate, I'm sure. Maybe the saddest part, for me, is how few people know that the world's most famous transman is also an Asian man.

But with the increased publicity masculine self-identified folks are getting these days, we have increasing opportunities to create a new idea of masculinity. Thomas Beatie is Asian! Spread the word! It's not a white thing! We've been around forever! The absence of a mainstream stereotype of transmen of color means that we get to set the tone ourselves. This very article—and in a broader sense, this book—is doing exactly that: shaping the idea of who we are, by us and for the world. Ambitious? Yes. Worthwhile? Definitely.

Talk Derby to Me

Uzi Sioux

I was incredibly nervous showing up to my first roller derby meat practice. It wasn't the roller-skating itself that scared me, although it should have. It was the thought of being surrounded by dozens of other women whom I might in the future have to skate with—or against. I had no idea what they would they think of me. I kept imagining being treated like a freak. I don't feel like I should have to disclose that I am transgender unless I choose to do so, but that doesn't mean I don't constantly worry about whether people might question my gender.

Practices were so tough that nobody had time to care about my gender identity, and I lost all hesitation about playing an all-women's sport. It was just too fun and crazy ever to give up. We practiced in an empty concrete parking garage full of potholes, oil slicks, and huge concrete columns. If you lost your footing, took a turn too sharp, skated over a pothole, or otherwise lost control, it was likely you'd either ram into a column or scrape a whole bunch of skin off your body from falling on the concrete or rubbing against a pillar. I definitely lost some skin off my arms and once on my knee when my kneepad slipped.

I skated in that garage for almost three months before I passed my first assessment and thus was allowed to practice indoors on a wooden floor with the league. The skating surface can make a huge difference, and let me tell you, no two are more different than concrete and slick wood floor. I was slipping and sliding all over the place that first day. Regardless, it was amazing to finally skate with the more than fifty rollergirls who were officially in the league.

I quickly spotted a few skaters who stood out above the rest and whose style I wanted to emulate. I have always been a competitive, athletic person, and I love having strong competitors or role models to challenge me. Pre-transition, I played soccer and practiced ice skating, cross-country running, rowing, weightlifting, and martial arts on men's teams or surrounded primarily by men. Yet the rollergirls were some of the greatest athletes I had ever seen, male or female, and they inspired me more than anyone else ever had. I became a lot less self-conscious about my muscular upper body, which to a lot of people is "unattractive" on a woman. Rollergirls get major respect for being buff, and there definitely are some pretty built girls on my league. The first promotional event I ever went to for my league featured an arm wrestling contest for prizes, and I got to see veteran rollergirls vying for first place, tournament-style.

While things were going very well for a while training with the league as a meat skater, about three months into my derby career I had a major setback in my training. Recovering from breast augmentation surgery, I couldn't come to practice for two weeks and was in incredible pain from all the muscle in my chest that the surgeon had moved around. I tried to keep it all secret, including wearing really baggy t-shirts to practices so people would "forget" my cup size. I only told one person on the league about it, a jammer for my future team, and to my surprise she was very supportive. One of her teammates was planning a breast augmentation too. I would never have guessed that possibly the most bad-ass rollergirl on our league, the one who had broken five bones on other girls, might have been uncomfortable with her natural cup size, just as I had. I no longer felt so different from the other girls on the league. I no longer felt guilty or lacking in self-esteem for wanting larger breasts.

After the two weeks of recovering from surgery, I was left with only two weeks to prepare for the upcoming assessment that would determine if I could become a full league member. I failed. Upset, I fell into a depression for a few months. I would remain a meat skater, which meant that I wouldn't get to be on a team and wouldn't be able to attend about half the league's practices.

There are two types of rollergirls—meat skaters and league skaters. As a meat, I was constantly forgotten or ignored by league skaters. Shy and guarded, I didn't do much other than show up and skate. I gave people the impression that I didn't want to be friends with anyone, and so few people reached out to me. I pushed everyone away because I was afraid of what they might think of me if they knew me (and my past) better.

The one person who saw through me was the team captain of the most successful team on the league. She saw the potential in me as a skater, but she needed to make sure I could be social and able to work with a team. I saw from the start that she wanted to draft me, so I definitely took her advice on being more social to heart.

About five months into my derby career, I passed the final assessment. I was drafted immediately by the captain who had been such a big help to me. Since then, she has become like a mother to me, nagging me when I skip practice, encouraging me to take on more challenges, and constantly pushing me harder.

With my new home team I started feeling a sense of family that extended even to the members of my team I barely knew. They made the effort to reach out to me and make me feel welcome, even though I was still afraid to reach out to some of them. I became close to a lesbian couple on my team, and I knew from conversations with them that they were aware of transgender issues. I finally took the plunge and came out to them at a skate rink one day. They were completely supportive and promised not to mention it to others. It was a huge relief to feel unburdened of what had been a burning secret for six months and to have other rollergirls to talk to that understood what it felt like to be queer, even if they weren't transgender themselves.

My first couple of derby bouts were huge successes, and I quickly became one of my team's best rookies. I'm a very small girl. I'm also a very fast skater with really good balance and agility, making me perfectly suited to be a jammer. Jamming is fun because you're the one responsible for scoring points for your team, but it also means that every single blocker on the other team is trying to knock you down or out of play.

After I took a particularly vicious pounding one bout, a rumor began circulating that the other team had made it key to their strategy to target me specifically. One day after practice, my captain took me aside and said that someone had made an anonymous complaint to the Board of Directors that I had an "unfair advantage" playing roller derby as a transgender woman and that the Board should investigate my hormone levels and surgical history.

My team rallied around me, and the Board agreed that no one should be forced to disclose private medical information to satisfy the discriminatory suspicion of one individual. The complaint was rejected. I was relieved to know that so many people had my back even on such a touchy subject as being a transgender athlete. In addition, no one asked me to come out, which was again a very positive sign. Several months later, my team appointed me as a representative to the Board, where I have had the honor of helping to ensure that everyone on the league can feel the sense of community and family that has been so important to my experience as a rollergirl.

Many of us rollergirls bond over wanting to feel feminine yet also liking the feeling of being tough, aggressive, and independent. Having grown up conforming somewhat to hegemonic masculinity, it is hard sometimes for me to separate out the tough girl I want to be from the tough guy I used to have to try to be. As a rollergirl, my feminine toughness no longer confuses me. I am surrounded by dozens of tough, feminine women all the time. Even my really loud voice becomes an asset; I receive frequent compliments on how I well I can rally my team and call a league meeting to order.

I have enjoyed growing into my skin as a rollergirl, both on and off the track. But more than anything, it is skating and bouting that I love. I wouldn't train two to three hours a day, five days a week, if I didn't care about being the best derby player I could be. In my roller derby career, I regularly play in front of enormous crowds of over a thousand people. In my first season, I was voted MVP at one bout by my team, and at the end of that season the league recognized me as runner-up for the award of Best Jammer. At the beginning of this season, I was accepted onto the travel team comprising the best skaters from all of the home teams. I am also now on the Board of Directors, a leadership position with responsibilities which are much more than I would have had the self-confidence to take on when I first joined the league.

And just the other night, in the same bar in which I first found out about the sport, a girl came up to me, addressed me by my derby name, and told me how great I had skated the previous weekend. It's not super-stardom yet, but who knows what it could lead to in a few years? I know of a few leagues that already have trading cards. . . .

Seeworthy

E.S. Weisbrot

It began the first time as a single theft. The gait of a man as he walked down the narrow tunnel toward the subway train. I fixed my gaze on it until I had it. And then I took it. He never noticed and it seemed he had forgotten he was using it at all, that walk so full of rawness and power, sheer aggressive forward motion. In me, it propelled my body up the platform and confidently onto the next train car.

The next time it was an elderly woman talking with her hands. Like twin birds, escaping from her limbs. I was transfixed and watched with single-point focus until I captured those winged things in my mind and felt my fingers take flight. She never saw me, no one saw me take them. In the end they were one of my most valued treasures, and I never felt a shred of guilt over the crime.

I stole only from those who knew not what they had. Sailed on bodies, bodies made mostly of water, the steel girders encased in flesh, each one rich with the bounty of identity, overwhelming in their possibilities. Crooked smiles, gentle smiles, mean smirks, painful grimaces, millions of vocal tones, thousands of styles of hair, a rippling laugh, an ambiguous gesture. I took so many things. I took the incognizant way of being and made it thoughtful. Each one I considered as I hauled it onboard and let the wind carry me by. Each one I valued for its gendered poignancy. Each one for what it had been unconsciously in the world, what it would be for me.

It didn't happen quickly but eventually, I became a cacophony. All the different pieces became music and the music became noise and the noise became something else. Something loud. The noise became loud like freedom and the freedom reeked of the destabilization of all that surrounded me. Reeked of the world changing. People began to notice. The questions were hushed, wondering about the way I wore my pants but then also that look to my face and that particular air about me. Wondering about that face, made up of so many gendered trinkets, a curio cabinet of found objects, dissected objects of human art. Curious about the combinations, they were interested in my collection. It wasn't long before it was an inquisition, before there were accusations. Someone recognized my posture in the corner bodega and shoved me like a sack of beans they wanted to see spill over and reveal its contents. "Pasticcio!" "Imposter!" "Thief!" "The way you are is not your own!" My blurred lines were suddenly too gray, my intelligently crafted, unintelligible assembly of parts and pieces was in danger. They felt the uncanny in the elements and were uncertain about just what to do with the whole. They knew not what to make of me because I was made of them.

And so I ran. I had tasted what tomorrow was, escape, tasted the breakdown of it all, the salt, the sea, the salt of that water. Alone, and bereft, I knew they would ultimately take my bounty away from me. I could not keep my treasures, I could not keep this me in this world.

I released them. Every one. The steps, the winks, the tones and the gestures. The moans and the positions, each demeanor, charm, and role. I abandoned the scraps of stolen language, squeezing out the emotions and grunts and pulling out the postures and the personalities. Some I let fly out through the screen, some I buried where they most belonged. Others just disappeared and when I felt like crying, or was filled with rage, I released that too, back to that person from whom it had been coveted.

By the time they found me, I was long gone and they hardly suspected anything by looking at me. Me; archaeopteryx, sponge, future. They asked me a few simple questions; where I had been on this day, that day, "Have you seen this person?" "Do you recognize this gender pirate?" "This thief who has made such a mess of the way things are?" A picture was held up, the image showing how I had been only moments before: a canvas awash with everything and nothing, no specific thing but all of it all at once. When I said I hadn't seen anything, they left, leaving only the ending behind.

And in the remaining silence, in the lingering, my eyes scanned to the window and the muffled voice of the person talking effusively on a phone just beyond the dusty glass pane. A beginning. Of everything.

interlude

We are two trans-bodies in motion, resisting description, definition, language not out of defense, but out of consequence. We do not harbor a private truth. We remain necessarily indecisive about the shape of "us"—but we are careful not to become estranged in our namelessness. We create embodiment not by jumping out of our skins, but by taking up a stitch in our skins, by folding and tying a knot in ourselves. Our bodies are drawn through themselves—neo-vaginas are made from originary penises or skin grafts, and trans-cocks emerge from testosterone-invigorated clitorises. There is no division, but continuity between the physiological and affective responses of our different historical bodies. The important distinction is not the binary one between wrong body and right body, or between fragmentation and wholeness. Indeed, changeability is intrinsic to our trans-bodies, at once our substance and our threshold. Our bodies are scarred, marked, and reworked into livable "gender trouble." We survive not because we become whole, but because we embody the reach and possibility of our layered experience. This is all to say, his body, my body, are bodies created out of necessity and ingenuity. We may desire some mythic wholeness, but what is truly intact for us, what we live, what we must be, are bodies pliant to a point, flexible within limits, constrained by language, articulation, flesh, history, and bone, even as all these elements remain in continuous unrest."

—Eva Hayward

And still we rise.

Part Five

Marsha P. Johnson :: ten suns the transformer ::

Tamiko Beyer

Marsha buys Sylvia a plate
of spaghetti first time
they meet   generous like that
at dawn find her asleep in the flower
district beneath heaped
tables petals stems
spring snow falling on her long
frame folded crushed
silk sleeping off the wild night
when the merchants pack
up for the day leave Marsha
with orchids for her hair
Marsha when she feels
it sheds all her clothes
sends them floating

on the Hudson offerings
to Neptune she says and sashays
down Christopher Street in glory
all and holy heels

INTERVIEWER: *You knew Marsha?*

FRIEND: On the train I'd run into her on the train she'd already be
on the train. And the homeboys would call her the transformer
because from Hoboken she'd leave as a man and as she pulled into
Christopher Street she'd become a woman.

INTERVIEWER: *What would she do, I mean she couldn't take off her
underwear. . . .*

funeral sobbing glittered mass
surges towards the piers
more home than any other
those concrete barriers those old boards
the only place to be all love for Marsha
like that   they fill up the street
and the sweating cops twitch hands
to batons but the chief
—some part soft hearing her off-key songs—
says *Marsha was a good*
queen give them the street
and so down Seventh Avenue to
the piers down
to the piers the procession
all love for the Saint of Christopher Street

FRIEND: She'd have like an oversized shirt with her dress bunched up inside of it. The dress come down and the Levis come off. Sometimes she'd leave the work boots. Work boots with a house dress. And then she'd you know pull a wig out of the bag and you know some kind of sash or something. They couldn't believe their eyes. She always kept a pair of scissors on her. They never bothered Marsha. They just called her the transformer.

INTERVIEWER: *And how did you feel? I mean in front of straight people and all?*

Marsha with a bullet
in her ass from a ripped
off pissed off john
P for *pay*
it no mind Marsha
photographed by Warhol
Marsha of the Hot
Peaches Review priestess
Marsha weaving her cosmology
across the Jersey skyline battered
in wild synaptic bursts Marsha says
I saw ten suns shining in the sky
gorgeous and freaked
like the end
of the world   I love my saints
darling but sometimes the visions

fish facts

    1. floating

    2. Hudson River near the piers

    3. after Pride

    4. police *investigation*

    5.—two phone calls—

    6. ruled her death a suicide

FRIEND: There was never any trouble. Never any trouble.

INTERVIEWER: *No one ever made any comments?*

FRIEND: No the conductors all knew. The conductors all knew and
    loved Marsha.

fist facts

we hold our own

post flyers for tips learn

some boys gave her

hell   near the piers

earlier that evening

Marsha at the club reads poems from a paper heart
glittered lips her voice a rasping sun

    you can be a leather angel

    on a sleek black Harley bike

    or a redhead shouting faggot

    or a dazzling giant

    you can lock yourself in a closet

    with a fine mink stole

but it really doesn't matter
   if you ain't got soul
she turns and the mirrors
on her headdress flash
stage lights flare to vision they
flood the camera's aperture
crowd whistles cheers drowns
her exit her clatter her hot her holy heels

                         *   *   *

Marsha P. Johnson was an important figure in
the New York City LGBT community from the 1960s
to the 1990s. An African-American transgender
activist and performer, she participated in the
Stonewall Rebellion and sang and recited poetry
with the Hot Peaches Review. At times homeless,
she co-founded Street Transvestite Action Revolu-
tionaries (S.T.A.R.) with her friend and fellow activist Sylvia Rivera. S.T.A.R. provided shelter, food,
and community for young transgender women
and drag queens living on the streets.

She-Male Rising

Shawna Virago

When I was eighteen, my band was invited to play a biker party. The party was at an old house off the highway, hidden by a thicket of trees. The house had a big dirt yard in front. You couldn't see the house from the highway and there were no neighbors around. My band got to crank up our amps pretty loud and not worry about noise ordinances. There were about a hundred people there, all kinds of desperado types in denim and leather. It was early evening and there was a barbeque going and several kegs. People were having a good time being boisterous, smoking, and drinking. I remember a slim-hipped naked go-go boy gyrating under a tree. My band was in the middle of playing a song at breakneck speed, when suddenly, like locusts, a swarm of police cars and paddywagons drove up the gravel driveway, jumping out with guns drawn and nightsticks slashing the air, attacking, yelling "Faggots, get down now!" People were panicked and scattering, screaming and running wildly in all directions. It was bedlam. It was senseless. I can still see one old grizzly butch dyke spraying the cops with a keg nozzle, limply splashing them with beer in a feeble attempt at self-defense, before being tackled and hogtied by three huge cops.

Somehow I had the wherewithal to grab my guitar and run into the house. I don't know why I ran in that direction; I guess my flight instinct was looking for the quickest way to escape the melee. The house seemed to be deserted and I ran down the hallway, into a bedroom, and got into the closet.

I was shaking with fear, trying to control my hard breathing. I tried to move deeper into the closet, behind some hanging clothes, and stepped on . . . a foot! Followed by a muffled "Ow!" Another person was in the closet! "Hello?" I whispered. "Hello?" a male sounding voice said. My hand brushed against him and touched skin. I realized it was the naked go-go boy. We were both dead still, trying to keep our fear in check and breathe quietly. No time for introductions. We could hear the bedlam outside, people screaming, damage being done, some motorcycles getting away. We held our breaths when we heard big boots stomp into the bedroom and look around. Fortunately whoever it was decided to leave. We let our breaths out and started to kiss. He put my hand on his cock and I pulled my jeans down and put his hand around mine. We both came about ninety seconds later. We didn't say anything about what we had just done. We both wiped our hands on some hanging clothes. After what seemed a long time, we realized the noises had died down, and we ventured from the closet, nervously peering out a window, shocked that no one seemed to be there.

Stepping onto the porch, we were met with chaos: things thrown about and overturned. Everyone was gone: the cops, the bikers, my bandmates, everyone. It was like surviving some sort of attack in a bunker and coming up when radiation levels are safe. I asked the go-go boy if he'd like to go hang out, but he surprised me and said he had to get back to his girlfriend. I wondered where his clothes were. I wondered if they might like a three-way. I put on a dab of lipstick. I hadn't transitioned yet. I quietly walked away.

When I got home I took a shower and put on some gospel music. I double checked that the door was locked. It had been an intense day. Angry cops, a closeted hand job, and rock n' roll. It felt like a cosmic thing: cops on one side and rock n' roll and sex on the other. Militant repression versus anarchic pure joy. I don't have to convince you where I stood or who was really the most lawless.

The biker party put into sharp focus which side of the divide I needed to live on. It pulled me out of the closet. Drawn to people living outside conventional boundaries, I took gender and music as the guiding posts of my life, my paths to freedom. Both have let me honor the most important parts of myself: a love of glamour; a passion for leftist politics; my outlets for love and anger; my calling to performing and songwriting; the place where I as a shy person could find myself both in the world and onstage, in a tumble of words and melodies; life.

I'm fortunate that I've had role models that gave me road maps to navigate gender and art with creativity and integrity. Role models that have helped me plunge into the pool of outlaw freedom and self-expression. Mentors who have helped me to fan the flames necessary to avoid punching the clock of conformity.

In the late '70s and early '80s I went to lots of punk rock shows. The band that I loved with fervor was the seminal Los Angeles punk band, X. They were majestic. Their music melted into my skin, a rush of high speed sonic roots music, which I could feel through my steel toed engineer boots, into my hips, into my mind. I was captivated, transformed to my depths. They had everything: politics, poetry, humor, rage, and a sensuality which inspired me to write songs based on those same elements. I was especially captivated watching X's amazing front woman, the poet Exene Cervenka. Watching Exene made me feel like I was getting away with something. She brought my mind and crotch alive with possibilities. With her 1930s fallen Hollywood starlet glamour and noir makeup, Exene was Barbara Stanwyck channeling Arthur Rimbaud, a tough gal pointing the way out of conformity of any kind. She gave me the keys to the queendom, the path to the bright lights of how to be my own person and not play by anyone's rules. If I could've just been a punk rock girl then! That would've been heaven.

When I started playing my music in San Francisco as an out transgender woman, back in the early to mid 1990s, I knew my gender would probably be the first thing the audience would see, and I was nervous about the reception I might get. Things were very different then. There was not a critical density of transgender or genderqueer folks in those days. Sometimes I'd perform with a band, but mostly I would do solo shows with just my guitar. I'd walk onstage and sweat my songs, anthems, odes, elegies, channeling the voices of sorrow, anger, sex, performing my truth, harmonica around my neck, shaking my hips, shaking my ass, suggesting a promise of more, bending spoons with my mind, card tricks, juggling knives, levitating beer bottles, long somatic soliloquies, and ribald odes. I'd finish with a somersault and walk offstage depleted, having given my all, panting, sweat pouring down my face.

It's vulnerable being read as female onstage. I think it was doubly so being read as a transgender woman, especially then. I worried. I got some serious flak. It made me protective, and it took me a few years not to care what the audience thought about my gender. I had to learn I wasn't there to be everybody's best friend. I wanted people to like my songs, sure, but that was it.

I played some shows at the CoCo club, a dyke community space, and I was largely accepted there (no small feat at the time). After one of my gigs, I made friends with a powerful transgender woman named Agatha, who was twenty years older than me. Like Exene, Agatha was an important mentor. We would take walks throughout the city and she'd say, "Shawna, you gotta be smart out there," tapping the side of her head. "But you also gotta be tough," she'd say and then show me some of her street fighting moves, including her favorite, the nipple grip. "Babe, it's as effective as a roundhouse kick! It makes a grown man cry for his mama!" She should've been a star in the Gorgeous Ladies of Wrestling. Some afternoons, her hands shaking from years of using crystal meth, she would point things out, like where the transgender strip clubs were in the 1960s and '70s, where she and her friends had lived, and where they had been harassed by cops. Walking with her was like having someone who could see ghosts left behind on a battlefield. She herself may have been a ghost. She was defiant and I admired her.

It's been a decade since my days with Agatha. She moved on to a horse ranch in the Dakotas and I've moved on too. I now publicly identify as a she-male. I'd put it on my driver's license if I could. I like the term, how it fits on my skin and rolls off my tongue. I started mentioning it at my shows the past couple of years. It's a declaration of self, a personal manifesto, to make explicit that I don't want to get swallowed up in the vortex of gender normativity. I like to think of transgender and gender variant people as gender adventurers, real swashbucklers who locate gender expression as a lifetime of creative and daring acts, in which transition never ends. I'm a lady and a she-male: I like to think of that as a big genderfuck.

One of my other great punk mentors, Joe Strummer of the Clash, coined a term the "Punk Rock Police," which he used to describe self-appointed arbiters who judged other punks for wearing clothes or playing music that they deemed not punk rock enough. For Joe Strummer, punk rock was his freedom, and he didn't appreciate the punk rock police censoring his self expression. Since coming out as she-male, I've encountered my own version of this phenomenon of self-appointed gatekeepers who sit in judgment of anyone they feel has strayed from the flock. I like to call them the Tranny Police, and like their punk rock counterparts, they have their fingers on the short hairs of everybody's business and they won't let go until everyone acquiesces to their conservative worldview of gender.

Like all fundamentalists who miss the good old days when they could stone people to death, they universalize their experience as representative for everybody. I've received several critical emails from the Tranny Police, expressing their anger at me for using the term she-male. These emails have a "How Dare You!" quality to them and have accused me of setting the movement back. The charge of setting the movement back I find amusing, since I think they're setting the movement back! I might not understand a transgender woman who identifies as heterosexual or as being born with Harry Benjamin Syndrome, but I wouldn't send a nasty email to her. Instead, I say, Go, Sister! Be Yourself! Just let me do the same.

Last week I played a show at a South of Market leather bar. I played mostly songs from my album *Objectified*, which chronicles a lot of my own gender struggles and empowerment. I also tried out a couple of new songs. Before my set, I was in line to use the bathroom. A silver haired Leatherman came out with his boy on a leash. Now it was my turn. I went in, locked the door, lifted up my mini-skirt, pulled down my fishnets and panties, and pissed in the rarely flushed toilet. My boots protected my feet from the small pool of mysterious dank liquids on the floor. I flushed the toilet. I am a lady, after all.

After my set I went out back to the patio and stood next to the fire pit. There was mist in the air. I saw two young genderqueers in each other's arms, both their eyes half closed, their mouths in slight smiles. Lots of people looked happy being out in community. I was about to chat with a friend, when a drunken non-transgender woman wearing a silver cap came up to me and asked, "Why are all your songs about being transgendered?" I responded by saying, "There's something in your teeth." About five minutes later a drunken transgender woman, a member of the Tranny Police who'd sent me angry emails, asked me, "Why don't you write songs about being transgendered?"

I wanted to tell her: Sister, life is short! Let's all take some deep breaths, fix our gaze on the future, let your lungs fill with rebellion. Let's be allies. Let's lift everyone trapped here in the bottom of the gender pond; let's feel our bodies rise and rise!

Instead, I pointed to the woman in the silver cap and said, "Go ask her."

Princess

Christine Smith

SHOT, STABBED, CHOKED, STRANGLED, BROKEN: a ritual for November 20th

Roz Kaveney

1

It could have been me.
I was young. I took risks.
True, I was white.
I hitched rides with guys
One at least was a killer
It could have been me.

It could have been me.
He came to my door
He showed me a badge
He pulled out a knife
He raped me. I felt
The hilt of the knife
I thought it was the blade.
It could have been me.

It could have been me.
They beat me in the street
They pummeled my breasts
And tugged at my wig
And said they would burn me
It could have been me.

It could have been me.
He drew up alongside
And asked me to ride
And knew who I was.
He followed my cab
And drove his car at me
It could have been me.

2

They died
On the streetcorner with the streetlight that blinked
With the rubbish bin dented by a passing car
Among bricks and bent girders
On the waste ground behind the convenience store
In the car park behind the bar where the toilets flooded
And the johns were bad men. Or in bed
Their own bed where they thought they were safe.
They died where people who die by violence die.

They died because
—Of course, there's no because. Just stupid whys
They died for smiling the wrong way

They died because god told someone gay things need to die
They died because they answered back
Or would not be called out of their names
Or let his hand go there between their legs
Or went on a hot date and told him and he didn't believe them until he did.
They died of other people's stupid violent hating ways.

The ones who died
The ones we know about
Thirty a year—that's more than two a month.
Handsome young transmen murdered in their pride
Duanna, Angie, Kelly, and the rest
Iraqis with their long hair shaved away
Our sisters and brothers
Thirty of them
Dead

3

When people die
Their smiles are taken from us
Who might have seen them
And smiled back.
Their songs are taken from us
Who might have heard
And listened and been glad.
Their stories are remembered
By us, on this day
And always.

Proof

Bo Luengsuraswat

Growing up, I was a real tough secret agent. I climbed trees, ran up mountains, and jumped waterfalls. I made weapons, played with fire, and got myself into countless accidents. Knocking my front teeth down my throat with an eight-foot bamboo stick while trying to high jump over a neighbor's fence and losing my virginity in a threesome accident with a bike seat and an electricity pole were nothing but ordinary occurrences. Rather than letting these bloody incidents scare me away from my secret mission, I took every lost tooth and scar to be the proof of my strength and determination. As an arm-wrestling champion, a whole-pizza eater, and a proud pyromaniac, I felt that nothing could stop me from conquering the world. I desperately wanted to show everyone my power, to redefine people's perception of me, to become recognized as the mighty Bo.

My secret mission continued to flourish through my teen years in a slightly different manner: I went from being a striker to a defender—from fearlessly acquiring scars to protecting myself from normative conditioning. On the verge of puberty, turning down help was part of my daily life. I refused to hold anybody's hand on the way out of the car, boat, or bus, and I was furious every time some random guy opened the door for me. If that happened, I would immediately step outside the door one more time, then reopen it myself, making sure that no one had stolen my precious masculinity. When my developing body began to betray me, my need to reaffirm my strength and masculine essence became absolute. As my childhood was quickly receding on the horizon and womanhood was approaching in no time, the ability to perform physical tasks on my own became my last resort to prolong the night.

Besides embodying and exhibiting physical strength, I learned not to cry and not to let anyone see my tears. For me, weeping in public was considered an act of dehumanization, as it shattered the image of the mighty Bo that I fought hard to maintain. I could not endure another consolation, another sweet talking to, another back-patting. One more hug and I would explode from shame and embarrassment. I restrained myself from expressing emotions. I did not let any pain affect my behavior. I truly believed that I was superhuman. I wanted to be the strongest person in the world. I wanted to be everything but a *girl*. That was my secret mission.

I love telling friends and strangers my off-the-hook childhood stories and heroic accomplishments. It feels great to relive the times of absolute rebellion, especially to remember how tough and energetic I was. Never once have I regretted anything I burned, any scars I have, or any unexpressed feelings. I could not be more proud of my survival efforts. I could not be more proud of my courageous actions. Most importantly, I could not be more proud of my strength.

While this might sound like a typical childhood that any masculine-identified person like myself might have experienced, it by no means serves as proof of anything now. Here I am, at twenty-three, experiencing a drastic decline in my physical ability and emotional stability due to multiple chronic illnesses. Hardly able to climb stairs and hold back tears, I am no longer the superhuman that I once was. My daily ritual has changed from confidently denying help to seeking every bit of assistance I can get, whether a hand to hold a door for me to limp through or a shoulder to cry on. These new corporeal limits have significantly shaped my spiritual self. No longer can I afford more scars and bruises. No longer can I inhale hurtful feelings and exhale only a stern face. No longer can I rely on my strength and ability to cast off others' damaging perception of me. The image of the mighty Bo has completely faded into my memory and is now contained in the stories I recite.

My declining health hits me like a slow heartbreak, but the reminders of my lost strength tackle me like a series of thunderbolts. I have gradually, incomprehensibly, become estranged from the body I once inhabited. My shoulders ache every time I attempt to lift a twenty-pound desk by myself, the same desk that I easily picked up from a trash alley a few years ago; my lower back throbs after half a mile of walking, less than a quarter of the distance that I used to jog painlessly everyday; and my stomach now cries when more than two big slices of pizza have passed through my digestive tract. I can barely recognize and accept this new, tender body as mine. The harder I try to recover my lost self, the harder my body crashes. The more I hold on to my lost abilities, the more intense the sense of failure I experience. Letting go of that third slice of pizza is like letting go of my victorious past. Hunting for walking assistance and asking strangers to hold doors for me were things I swore I would never do in this lifetime. Angry, frustrated, and hopeless, I reluctantly observe the last bit of moonlight disappearing from the sky.

The dawn of womanhood frighteningly greets me, "You're welcome, lady." Unable to protect myself from those piercing words and shut people up by showcasing my strength, I am severely suffocating. In the end, all the years of body-torturing rites and compulsive strength-affirming habits back-fire on me. Helplessly watching my buff biomale friends and macho movers enthusiastically march up and down multiple flights of stairs with big pieces of furniture and my heavily packed boxes, I feel left out of this "Man Power" movement. What proof do I have to secure my masculinity at this point? Does my vulnerable physique simply reaffirm others' perception of me as female? How can I embody and express a masculine gender identity without the strength associated with maleness? These are the questions that I constant-ly ask myself, wishing that one day I will no longer endure misrecognition as a consequence of my deteriorating body and wavering spirit.

Gauging my feelings and energy levels in order to know when to disap-pear from the public eye has become necessary for my survival, as I feel the need to create an illusion of strength in order to prevent further damage to my sense of self. Under critical conditions, once again, my secret mission prevails. But now, my goal is merely to live through each day. Because the psychological tension that I experience significantly hampers my ability to move through the world, every simple task turns into a burden for me. No longer can I blindly bike home from school, relentlessly carry on a conver-sation, or easily finish my meal. Survival for me means consciously forcing everything to happen, whether it be anxiously deciding which path to travel, constantly pausing during conversations to weave thoughts into words, or forcing every bite of food down my throat for the sake of health.

Here I am, the mighty Bo.

I realize now that although I do not have a normatively capable body to prove my strength, my breathing self is nonetheless a sign of deter-mination. Painfully swallowing each bite of rice in order to survive when my stomach has given up on food is comparable to gulping down gigantic slices of pizza in order to challenge the popular conception of what female bodies can do and to legitimize my genderqueerness. Watching others' surprise and hearing their disbelief when I tell them the amount of food I used to eat is as rewarding as observing my body live through each day. I have come to understand that strength is a relative concept, and that mightiness is still within my reach.

Seeing how my desire to give proof of my masculinity leads to feelings of inadequacy and failure, I have learned a hard lesson: There is no such a thing as a stable sign of masculinity that I can rely on to validate my sense of self. Paying attention to every moment of my being has helped me understand how much strength, energy, and ability it takes to function normatively in the world, from walking through a door to eating to interacting with others. All of these things illustrate that gender identification unwittingly depends on the privileges of ability. Is masculinity the ability to endure danger, lift a twenty-pound desk by oneself, or suppress emotions? Is strength necessarily a marker of masculinity? Is my only masculine value in what I can endure?

As much as I want to say no to these questions, I cannot deny the traumatic effect of having the independence I had used to define my masculinity stripped right out of me. It departed with well-meaning strangers and friends who assisted me with labor-intensive tasks, helped me finish my meals, and were there to comfort me through difficult times. Learning to accept change and loss allows me to appreciate my remaining ability and fluctuating psychological being. Nevertheless, I am continuously, haunted by the ideology of gender that threatens to associate my declining physical strength and emotional hypersensitivity with femininity and womanhood. No matter how much I try to subvert gender norms or redefine the idea of strength, I can never rid myself of the fear of misrecognition. No matter how entitled I feel in this body, I struggle to be seen.

I am still hesitantly seeking a shoulder to cry on. But perhaps that, too, is a kind of strength.

The Voice

Joy Ladin

It's a cliché of male puberty, and for many thirteen-year-old bar mitzvah boys, a painful one: the cracking voice that wobbles unpredictably between childhood and adulthood. In the past three years, I'd heard my son's voice creak, crack, and finally plunge to a booming, gravelly bass that made him sound older than his fourteen years. My son was both shy and proud of his new voice, as he was of the suddenly adult-size body that he found himself inhabiting, the muscles bulking out his arms and shoulders, the fine curling hair making its way down his cheeks, across his lips, over his chin. Without any apparent effort, his body was becoming a man's.

Over the same three years, albeit with a great deal of effort, my body had been moving in the opposite direction. High-intensity lasers at precisely calibrated frequencies had burned out follicles my own male puberty had stimulated. My rough red-brown beard and mustache were gone, most of the remaining hairs pale and increasingly fine. My chest and back hair were almost eliminated, though I still had to shave my legs and arms every day or two. My upper body contours had become slimmer as testosterone-stimulated muscle broke down, my skin finer, softer—and more vulnerable to varicose veins and cellulite. Even in the androgynous, shape-concealing jeans and baggy shirts I wore with my children, strangers generally took me as a woman.

But when I spoke to my children, it was in the voice they had always known—the deep Daddy voice, the voice of our shared past. As female-to-male transsexuals take testosterone, their vocal cords lengthen and their voice boxes expand, lowering pitch and shifting timbre to masculine ranges. But estrogen has no effect on a male-to-female transsexual's voice.

For most of my life, information about transsexuality was hard to come by. I would hunt surreptitiously through libraries and bookstores for anything that mentioned—well, people like me. I found very little, mostly personal testimonials that didn't mention the practicalities of transition. By the time I started to research transition in earnest, the world had changed. I typed "transsexual transition" into a search engine and there they were: hundreds, if not thousands, of websites offering transsexuals for sexual pleasure, hormones and prostheses to aid cross-dressing, discussion boards, links, true life stories of transition, before and after pictures, "find the transsexual among the real women" games, dating services, how-to advice on dressing like a woman, walking like a woman, shopping like a woman—and, here and there, factual information about transition.

Apparently, transition was simple. All I had to do was suppress my testosterone level and elevate my estrogen level, and even my thick, hairy, middle-aged body would undergo a belated female puberty. My metabolism would slow, because testosterone burns calories, while estrogen encourages the body to store fat. My endurance would decrease, because testosterone helps the body absorb oxygen during physical exertion, and estrogen doesn't. My upper body muscle would break down, my fat would build up, and fat cells would migrate from masculinity-defining sites like cheeks and belly to femininity-defining sites like breasts, buttocks, and hips. My center of gravity would shift downward from shoulders toward hips. My face would become thinner, my arms and shoulders more delicate. An extra layer of fat would build up beneath my skin, making it softer and smoother, and my body hair would become finer, lighter, sparser. My erections would become infrequent, then incomplete, then more or less stop, as my testes underwent what the medical sites charmingly called "hormonal castration."

It would be slow—like natural puberty, male-to-female puberty takes about six years—but, given a proper hormone replacement regimen, it would be inexorable, and by the end of two years, my body should "read" as female.

It sounded like heaven to me.

But there were three flaws in the heaven of hormonal feminization. Hormones wouldn't transform my genitals; as I'd known since childhood, only surgery could do that. Hormones wouldn't change my skeletal structure; my hips would always be too narrow and my shoulders too broad. And hormones wouldn't change my voice.

The first two were daunting but expected. The last was devastating.

My voice was the one male part of me I didn't loathe, the most important part of my persona as a teacher and a poet, the one means I'd found to touch other people without being touched and thus physically reminded of the foreignness of the body they mistook for me. I had stopped exercising in my early twenties when I realized that muscle development emphasized the masculinity of my physique, but I kept working on my male voice, learning to exploit its depth (during my brief stint in a chorus, I was a bass) and resonance to sound honest, concerned, angry, soulful, playful, deadpan.

I learned to fill it with love when talking to my children and to fill it with contrition when talking to God. I learned to sound crisp and authoritative on business calls and tender and vulnerable when murmuring in the dark with my wife. Most importantly, I learned to think of that voice as me.

To live as a woman, I had to lose what I'd made of my voice and start from scratch. Rather than developing the natural qualities of my voice, I would have to learn to suppress and distort them. And somehow, through that process of suppression and distortion, I would have to create a voice that was as supple, as expressive, as authentic—that would feel as much like mine—as the voice I'd been grooming since it first began to crack. That seemed impossible. How could any other voice feel like mine, like an authentic expression of me?

I had always loved women's voices, but now I started to listen to them in a new way. It turned out that there were as many kinds of women's voices as there were women—lilting and husky, light as butterfly wings and heavy as honey, throbbing like a series of organ chords, piping like a slender shepherd's flute, brittle, broken, scratchy, maternal, sharp, sexual, ironic, naïve, yearning, trilling, breathy, breathless, cool, yearning. . . . In fact, there were more kinds of voices than there were women, because each woman had a repertoire of different voices at her disposal. I listened in awe as a voice used in laughing conversation with a friend morphed into the impatient tenderness of dealing with a needy child, the matter-of-fact superiority of telling a hapless husband something he should have known, and back to the ease of friendship. Men's voices, I realized, hew close to a single pitch; women's roam up and down the scale, and often in torrents of words in which I could hardly detect a breath. Some women's voices were so effortlessly gorgeous they broke my heart; some sounded like the aural equivalent of a bad haircut; but all instantly and unmistakably marked their producers as women.

It was clearly time for another Internet search.

When I typed "transsexual voice" into the search engine, in 2.2 seconds I had several thousand options. I worked my way through the list, culling what I could from each website. One detailed a list of vocal mannerisms that distinguish male and female speech in our culture (women, according to this website, speak faster, use their hands more, and emphasize the ends rather than the beginnings of words). One urged me to sing along with deep-voiced women singers; one suggested I speak along with—and even act out—female roles in Hollywood movies. I started singing and speaking along, talking faster, reminding myself to do something with my hands occasionally (I wasn't sure what), and articulating final consonants. None of those changes seemed to move me significantly along the gender spectrum. Reluctantly, I turned to the technical websites. One pointed out that women use a lot more air when speaking than men do. Another told me to cut out the chest resonance that men typically use to amplify their voices and direct my airflow to the small cavities in my head, as women do. A third gave step-by-step instructions as to how to nudge my voice pitch upward without breaking into falsetto, and offered to sell me sound analysis software that would tell me exactly how many cycles per second I was from reaching femininity.

My growing list of things to remember to do and not do when talking turned speaking into an exhausting and humiliating exercise; the only thing I was sure I'd learned was that every sound that came out of my throat proved I wasn't a woman.

I wasn't getting anywhere by imitating female NPR announcers, singing along with Sheryl Crow, or articulating the final "ng" of every gerund, and I didn't have the money for voice coaching or videos, so I turned to a free online how-to manual called "Finding Your Female Voice." The most encouraging part was the title: I loved the idea that I was "finding" a voice that was already female and already mine, rather than approximating others' voices. Less encouraging was the insistence that finding that voice would require me to do extensive voice exercises every day for the rest of my life, and to do them perfectly. I was willing to practice, but perfection was not an option. The manual envisioned a monk-like daily regimen that involved warm-ups, herb tea with lemon, and a safe, quiet, private place to sit that would enable me to maintain the good posture necessary for an unobstructed airstream. Since I was still living with my family, sleeping, working, and otherwise living on the couch, I did most of my exercises on my daily walks. Rather than sitting calmly and breathing steadily, I did endless sequences of vocalizations ("Ayo, Bo, Ko, Do, Eyo. . . . ") while striding uphill and down, pausing occasionally to play myself back on the cheap handheld recorder that always told me the same thing. Not only did I not sound female; to my ears, I barely sounded human.

But as days of vocalizing turned into weeks, and 15-minute practices turned into half hours, my voice started changing. I no longer had anything that could be called "my voice." The male voice I used with my family and at my job now seemed rough, barbaric, a hostile intrusion into my nascent sense of self rather than an expression of who I was. The rasp and rumble of air in my chest seemed like the intrusion of something foreign into my body. My male voice no longer connected me to others; it confirmed my utter isolation. I could feel the air moving in my throat, my mouth, in the cavities of my head as I spoke; I could shape it, direct it, increase and decrease amplitude, breathiness, resonance. The result was a new voice, or rather a series of new voices, that I practiced when talking to myself, on business calls, and with friends. These voices were strained, unreliable, and required constant thought and effort; the unfamiliar buzz of air in the small cavities in my head gave me headaches. My pitch was too low, except when it was too high, my resonance either faux operatic or barely there at all. Even when I talked to my closest friends, those who really knew what I was going through, I couldn't shake the sense that my voice was a caricature they listened to with pity.

But gradually, imperceptibly, my vocal gender was shifting. When I answered the phone at home, people often mistook me for my wife. When I made business calls, I was usually referred to as "ma'am." (On one call to my medical insurer, the woman helping me was convinced that I was a woman trying to conceal an unplanned pregnancy from an abusive husband.) Though the tape recorder assured me that my voice in no way resembled that of a genetic woman, I had accumulated enough female markers that strangers "read" my voice as female, if only because it sounded nothing like a man's.

That, it seemed, was the voice of my future, a voice estranged from masculinity but not yet, perhaps not ever, the voice of the woman I was struggling to become. That was the best I could do until a friend gave me something I was sure I could never afford—three lessons with a professional voice coach.

After the first five minutes of coaching, my teacher's friendly, respectful, unsparing critique made it clear that I had done an amazing but completely wrong-headed job of remaking my voice. The voice I worked so hard to produce was strained, artificial, and pumped up with so much excess resonance it was hard to make out the words I was saying. The voice exercises to which I was devoting an hour a day weren't getting me closer to finding my female voice—they were wearing my vocal cords out. On the plus side, those exercises had given me so much control over the mechanisms of my voice that I was instantly able to modulate airflow and resonance in response to my teacher's instructions. She adjusted my pitch downward, opened my air passages to increase breathiness, cut some of my head resonance and added a trace of the chest resonance I had eliminated months before. The result was a voice that sounded and even felt easy and natural. She didn't want me to sound like "a woman." She wanted me to sound like me.

The ease of that voice made it hard for me. My life had always been defined by discomfort with myself. The steps I had taken to find my female voice had increased that discomfort, reminding me, every time I opened my mouth to speak, of the difference between what I was and what I wanted to be.

But according to my voice teacher, the only way I could find my female voice was to realize that there was no difference between what I was and what I wanted to be. The voice of my future wasn't something to strive for, it was something to relax into, to accept in all its husky imperfection. It might feel like progress, but it was necessity. I would find my voice by speaking as myself.

The Role of Culture in Cleansing Gender Outlaws: The Lamal Ceremony of the Maasai, Kenya

Judy Wawira Gichoya and Priscilla Maina

Outlaws! A term that makes you think of social banishments, reject-ed persons, and a million other possibilities. I have fond memo-ries of the evenings during my childhood when stories were told to us by our grandmothers. This was the only way to pass on traditions as well as norms. There were many stories of outcasts, the moral to all of which was summarized as "the fate of those who have wronged the gods is to become an outlaw." I was born later, after the missionary work had westernized my village, but I did have a grandmother who had lived through it all and made it her goal to pass on the traditional culture.

Among most traditional African communities, the value of children and the role of supernatural powers in the balance of nature cannot be overemphasized. This is evidenced by beliefs that are common even in modern-day educated young Kenyans, who attribute conditions like mental illness and epilepsy to witchcraft or curses. Children are highly valued in the Maasai community and symbolize wealth and power for men, together with livestock and the number of wives. Many ethnographic studies refer to the importance of *social* rather than *biological* paternity of Maasai children. The sexual access of age-mates to each other's wives has been noted by several authors. A husband may urge a wife to be impregnated by a certain age-mate of his, whom he admires either for his oratory skills, bravery, or certain physical qualities. These children are nevertheless understood to be and treated as his children, as any children he may sire on his age-mates' wives are considered to be their children in all social and kinship matters.

Gender in literal sense refers to being a man or a woman in society. The community then identifies roles and duties for each of the genders. Gender outlaws, therefore, have breached the unwritten "contract" of what duties and roles one should perform according to one's gender. Childbearing was, and still remains, a duty of women. Therefore barren women were thought to be cursed or bewitched, and are treated as outlaws in their gender. We wish to discuss the way in which the Maasai culture has developed ritual to "cleanse" the outlawed barren women using the *lamal* ceremony. The information obtained herein was as a result of qualitative interviews with key community informants, specifically Maasai elders.

The *lamal* ceremony is a ceremony where women from the Maasai community who have not given birth, and women who want more children, get blessings and thus are able to conceive from other men besides their husbands. It is carried out between the months of September and December every five years and its timing is a well guarded secret until the last minute.

PREPARATIONS

Women who do not have children meet secretly over some time; at this point this is kept a secret even from their husbands. After arranging the logistics of the ceremony, the women invite women from the village who do have children. They request one woman per household, usually the first wife, who is believed to have a lot of experience with the ceremony. At this point the ceremony is no longer a secret, and everyone in the community approves of it, including their husbands. One of the women said: *"It takes months of work to prepare for these ceremonies, so the exact date of such an event is rarely known until the last minute. It is a secret."*

THE CEREMONY

The women visit a witch doctor, *oloiboni,* a leader with the power to predict the future, who chooses the best site for the ceremony. This is usually the homestead of an Elder who has many children, and who is known to be a good person who has never killed or fought with anyone, or been cursed. This is where the women build their *manyatta,* a collection of houses, for the ceremony, and start living in them. During the day the women walk in groups from one household to another, asking for money or sheep to be used during the ceremony. The money collected is used to buy red ochre. The sheep are collected in the *manyatta* and are used as food during the ceremony.

During the women's stay in the homestead, they have indiscriminate unprotected sexual intercourse with men who come to this homestead to drink beer and have sexual intercourse. As the women walk around in groups, they look for young men, especially those they have always admired, and have forced sexual intercourse with them. The group gets hold of the man and leaves the interested woman with him. This is generally acceptable; the women are not answerable to their husbands for what they do during the ceremony.

The women prepare *enaisho*, traditional beer used for blessing the women.

The witch doctor is called again and seeks divine intervention on how the women without children have *"wronged the gods."* The witch doctor is accompanied by Maasai elders. The beer is put in a gourd, *enkukuri*. The women make a frame from grass at the gate of the *manyatta*. The witch doctor pours the beer on the grass when all the women are in the *manyatta*, they come out through the frame, and the beer pours over them, carrying blessing.

The women are then required to go straight home and have intercourse with their husbands after the ceremony so as to get the blessings. If the woman sleeps elsewhere, she does not get the blessing. However, not all the women bear children after the ceremony; some have to perform the ceremony over and over again. The women with children spend the night in the homestead and go back home the next day.

PURPOSE OF *LAMAL*

This ceremony is intended to enable women who do not have children to conceive. It is also intended to help women who have children to bear children from other men, especially those whose families they have always admired, especially those with very successful children.

It is believed that if a husband is angry, he could curse his family, causing the death of all his children. This curse, however, would not affect children he has not fathered. One of the women in the focus group discussion said:

It is also believed that children who are from other men do better than the man's biological children, as the fathers who bring them up dislike them and make them perform the hardest chores. This, it is believed,

makes them more hardworking in an attempt to gain his love and accep-
tance; thus, they become more successful.

We hope that the above description is helpful to understand the method Maasai culture has developed for cleansing gender outlaws. In the past, the traditional culture set the conditions for one to be outlawed. At the same time, the tradition provided the means to return an outlawed person back to the community. Those who are outlaw to their gender can participate in the ceremonies and remove the stigma of the outlaw from themselves and their families.

shooting s(t)ar

Amir Rabiyah

You slip off my plastic coat & hat. Fill
my hard belly insides. Dose me a
perfect line. Wipe off the week. Mark
the spot. Save me a place on your
skin. Call me vicious before my steel
sticks you. Brother, I was born to
transform you into an archer. I crave
the sound of go. Pull. Pull. Release. I
am your hot flash spinal arrow —→ my
quiver guides flight. I puncture your
muscled wall. I exodus old body. You
exodus old body. We blood tangle. I
race against your pulse. Kiss your
cells till you sweat constellations

Pilgrimage

Zev Al-Walid

Four years ago in Madinah, I sat on the soft carpets in the Prophet Muhammad's mosque. The mosque was cool despite the arid desert heat, a building imposing in its beauty, crafted almost entirely out of white marble, with air conditioning that kept the temperature bearable inside. The spaces in between pillars were lined with coolers full of water from the Well of Zamzam, enough to quench the thirst of every pilgrim who came in to pray.

Memories of my last Umrah flooded back: of taking a quick shopping break to buy my first leather vest, trying it on in front of the perplexed storekeeper and pretending it was for a brother who was exactly my size; of the man at the rotisserie chicken shop who placed my change in my palm and then caressed his way up my sleeve, which made me feel so icky that I had to shower before praying; and of the rowdy teenage boys on an escalator who yelled obscenities at me when I walked past them. I was furious then, but this time, I was oddly calm.

Only my face peeked out of the huge, white, tent-like garment encasing my body. Underneath it, I wore my usual clothes—jeans and a t-shirt with an inverted pink triangle on it over boxer briefs and a chest binder. As an out and proud queer, many of my t-shirts are from queer events, marches, and fundraisers. I hadn't picked this one out intentionally for its loaded imagery, but I was glad to have a queer symbol next to my skin, my big white tent keeping my self-expression safe from judging gazes.

This would be my second time performing the Umrah, or lesser pilgrimage, in the holy cities of Makkah and Madinah. Some eight years back, on a similar trip, I had been struck by the decidedly unfeminist realities of modern day Saudi Arabia. As an awkward and androgynous fourteen-year-old, I disliked having to cover my body and hair, I loathed needing a male escort to enter the country, and I despised having to pray apart from the men.

Four years later, I walked through the women's entrance of the mosque without complaint. I had started hormone replacement therapy three weeks prior, on the vernal equinox, and I was praying and meditating on my movement from woman to man. My trip was a farewell: the last time I would go before the Almighty in female garb. I wanted spiritual closure, but I also sought insight on how to be a Muslim man, a subject about which I knew next to nothing.

That morning, as I walked out from my hotel room in a state of ihram, or ritual purity, I stared enviously at the male pilgrims wearing only two white towels. How I wished I could be seen that way, instead of hiding behind layers of fabric draped over me, with only my face visible to the world. A pang of loneliness set in, and I scanned the crowd for a man with bilateral chest scars, men with breasts, short men with hips. I wanted to be able to run up to him and say, Hey, I'm trans, too. I want to come back post-transition, like you. And I need you to tell me that I can do it, that it isn't impossible. That you have survived.

In a sea of thousands of pilgrims, I found several men with scars that could have told any number of stories, I spotted dozens of men with breasts, and I saw hundreds who were short. I was glad to see such biological variance even when gender roles were so clearly defined. But on the other hand, I wanted so badly to mark myself as queer, as trans, and to be able to recognize others within the crowd. I wanted to tear off my outer layer and walk around in my blatantly queer t-shirt. I wanted someone to notice the outline of my lycra binder underneath my clothes and to see who I was inside.

Several years later, I would have to remove more than just the outer layer of my clothing to be seen as anything other than a rather unremarkable looking stocky guy. But evidence of my transition isn't just written on my skin. It's also apparent from looking at my passport, which bears an incongruent name and sex marker, as well as an old Umrah visa that serves as evidence of my faith. Between my appearance and my papers, I tend to arouse suspicion at international borders, through which I travel frequently for both work and play—and it's anyone's guess whether I will be stopped for being a man traveling with a woman's documents, for being brown-skinned, or simply for having Arabic writing in my passport.

All of these things have actually happened. After a ten PM to four AM layover in Changi International Airport in Singapore, I dragged myself to the transfer counter, which was just opening, to get my boarding pass for the next segment of my journey. Before we even got in line, every traveler's documents would be checked by a security guard to make sure that ze had a valid ticket for the next segment of hir journey. When my turn came, I handed him my passport and flight details, and without any explanation, he asked me to wait. It was a good thirty minutes before his supervisor arrived.

She turned to confer with the security guard, who proudly told her—in Malay, which is a language I speak—that he had caught a man impersonating a woman so that he could use a stolen passport.

"Excuse me, Ma'am," I said—in Malay—to the supervisor, putting on my Polite And Agreeable Young Man persona, usually very useful for getting me through bureaucratic situations. "Is there a problem here?"

She flipped through my documents, gave me a quick once-over, and, faced with the prospect of having to bring up the embarrassing topic of why I didn't look like a woman, and in her native language no less, she opted just to give me back my passport and wave me through the line.

Avoiding embarrassment isn't a value held dear by the officers of the United States Bureau of Citizenship and Immigration Services, though. On a recent trip to San Francisco, after the routine questioning and fingerprinting, I was sent off to Secondary Processing.

This time, I was sharing the room with people who were bearded, wearing headscarves, or who were just brownskinned. Among us were a Canadian couple, dressed like consultants, with plans to visit Yosemite; a large family with strollers, baby slings, and sulking tweens who had been separated from their iPods; and a professor from India who was about to present a paper at a conference. There was one white couple; they were in the process of importing two large dogs. As I waited for my case to be resolved, the officers called other people to the counters—Patel, Ali, Mendez—and then it was my turn.

"Why," asked the officer, "were you in Saudi Arabia?" I informed him that I was a Muslim and that I had been on my Umrah, and before too much longer, I was escorted to a small room, all silver and shiny inside, as though every surface within it had been coated in aluminum sheeting. A small sign on the outside designated it the Pat Down Room. My luggage awaited me there.

My palms sweated as I walked in. A thorough pat down, or worse, a strip search. I didn't know if being seen as trans as well as Muslim in this particular context would make things better or worse for me. Either way,

I was scared, and then paranoid that my fear would make me look guilty, even though I hadn't done anything wrong.

The officers asked me to open my bags and pull out items one by one. It felt weird showing them my boxer briefs, especially my Batman underpants. Usually those only get seen by people with whom I am very close, and whom I like a great deal.

At some point, another officer came into the room to inform me—without a word of apology—that I was free to go. As soon as I could shove all my stuff into my suitcase and force it shut, I hightailed it out and turned on my cell phone so I could apologize to my poor friend Jess, who had promised to pick me up at the airport three hours earlier.

On another trip, as I was entering Canada, the border guard started off with an apology. She scrutinized my passport for some time, and then could contain herself no longer.

"Sorry," she said, "But are you aware of any mistakes in your passport?"

I told her that she might have noticed an inconsistency, in that my gender was listed as female.

"I'm a transsexual," I said. "But my country has some work to do on making appropriate accommodations when people transition from one gender to another."

"I can see that," she said, shifting uncomfortably. "You'd be able to change your documents here in Canada, too, but not just willy nilly. You'd have to at least *try* to be a woman first." She emphasized her point with gestures of extravagant cleavage.

My jaw must have hit the floor, or at least the counter of the immigration checkpoint. I explained that I was a transsexual man, that I had been born female but since moved away from that identity, and that under no circumstances would my country of origin allow me to change my documents from female to male.

"Well then," she said, pursing up her lips in disapproval. "That's not very nice of them, now, is it?"

"No," I said. "It really isn't."

And with a huff, she stamped my papers, and I exited to the baggage claim area of Toronto's Pearson International Airport.

People often ask me what it's like being trans. "Is it difficult?" they ask, perhaps expecting stories of family tension, of losing friends, or of physical danger. The fact is that I am not just trans—I am trans and queer and brown and Muslim, and I cannot separate the impact of any one of those things—positive or negative—from all of the others.

And furthermore, the truth is that I lead a blessed life. My family of origin has always loved me, and they are not unwilling to learn new ways of expressing this love for me. I live among a great band of queers and outlaws and troublemakers whom I have chosen as my tribe. I have a graduate degree and a professional environment in which my contributions are recognized. I used to think my life would be perfect if only I could have an apartment with central heat and AC and a kitchen with an oven and dishwasher and now I even have all of that. Most days, I can barely get started counting my blessings.

But it is true that my legal paperwork does not match my life. I do not travel in groups because of the high probability that I will cause delays at international borders. I cannot travel on business unless my travel companions, the person booking the ticket, and the person authorizing the funds for travel are all aware that I am trans. I have declined international consulting projects because I'd known the people responsible for sponsoring my visa to be transphobic or even merely ignorant of trans issues.

Despite all this, my feeling about the challenges that have arisen in my life is overwhelmingly one of victory. The person I have lived as for many years—the person I *am*—does not legally exist and cannot exist given the law in my country of citizenship. Regardless, I have lived, I have traveled, and I am in the process of getting my identity legally recognized via applying for citizenship elsewhere.

When I have that new passport in hand, I would like to apply for a Hajj visa, for permission to undertake the major pilgrimage, compulsory to all able-bodied Muslims who can afford it. I would like to go back to the Prophet's mosque in Madinah, not to say goodbye this time, but to say hello. I would like to be the man I was looking so hard for during my last visit, the man in two white towels with bilateral horizontal scars across my chest, chanting the pilgrim's prayer at the top of my lungs, which begins, "Labbaik Allah humma labbaik"—Here I am, oh Lord, here I am.

Cisgender Privilege:
On the Privileges of Performing Normative Gender

Evin Taylor

The latin prefix "cis," loosely translated, means "on this side," while the prefix "trans" is generally understood to mean "change, crossing, or beyond." Cisgender people are those whose gender identity, role, or expression is considered to match their assigned gender by societal standards. Transgender people are individuals who change, cross, or live beyond gender.

Privilege is the "cultural currency" afforded to a person or group of persons who are recognized as possessing a desired social or political characteristic. Privilege is the stability society affords us when we don't rock the boat.

Gendered privilege is the collective advantages that are accepted, most often unknowingly, by those who are not positioned in opposition to the dominant ideology of the gender binary. Simply put: A person who is able to live in a life and/or body that is easily recognized as being either man/male or woman/female generally needs to spend less energy to be understood by others. The energy one need not expend to explain their gender identity and/or expression to others is gendered privilege.

The following questionnaire was inspired by Peggy McIntosh's article "Unpacking the Invisible White Knapsack" (1988). This questionnaire is intended to inspire some insight into the privileges of those who are, for the most part, considered to be performing normative gender. It is certainly not an exhaustive list, nor can it be generalized to people in every social position. Gendered privilege is experienced differently depending on the situation and the individual people involved. Readers of this article are encouraged to adapt the questions to suit their own positioning and to come up with questions that can be added to the list.

1. Can you be guaranteed to find a public bathroom that is safe and equipped for you to use?
2. Can you be sure to find a picture of someone whose gender expression resembles yours somewhere on a magazine rack?
3. Can you be reasonably sure whether to check the M or F box on a form?
4. Can you be reasonably sure that your choice of checked box on such forms will not subject you to legal prosecution of fraud or misrepresentation of identity?
5. Are you able to assume that your genitals conform relatively closely to portrayals of 'normal' bodies?
6. Can you expect to find a doctor willing to provide you with urgent medical care?
7. Are you able to make a decision to be a parent without being told that you are confused about your gender?
8. Can you be confident that your health care providers will not ask to see your genitals when treating you for a sore throat?

9. Can you be confident that your health care providers will provide treatment for your health concerns without assuming that you chose to be ill?
10. Can you obtain a passport and travel without government employees asking explicit questions regarding your genitals?
11. Do people often act as if they are doing you a favor by using the appropriate pronouns for your gender?
12. Can you undress in a public changing room without risk of being assaulted or reported?
13. Are you able to discuss your childhood without disguising your gender?
14. Can you provide government identification without risking ridicule for your name or legal sex status?
15. Do you need to prove your gender before others will refer to you with your chosen name and pronouns?
16. Can you wear a socially acceptable bathing suit?
17. Does the government require proof of the state of your genitals in order to change information on your personal identification?
18. Are incidental parts of your identity defined as a mental illness?
19. Can you reasonably expect to be sexual with your consenting partner of choice without being told you have a mental illness?
20. Do other people consider your lifestyle a mental illness?
21. How many mental illnesses can be put into total remission through medical surgeries?
22. Can you expect that your gender identity will not be used against you when applying for employment?
23. Do your sexual preferences cause people to assume that your gender identity is mistaken?
24. Can you expect to be reasonably eligible to adopt children if you should choose to?

25. Do people assume that they know everything about you because they saw an investigative news episode about plastic surgery?

26. On most days, can you expect to interact with someone of a gender similar to your own?

27. Can you expect to find a landlord willing to rent to someone of your gender?

28. Do teachings about your national and cultural history acknowledge the existence of people of your gender identity?

29. Can you be sure that your children will not be harassed at school because of your gender?

30. Can you be sure that school teachers will not try to convince your children that their understanding of their family members' bodies is incorrect?

31. Are you able to use your voice and speak in public without risk of being ridiculed?

32. Can you discuss feminism with others without the appearance of your genitals being called into question?

33. Can you freely use checks, credit cards, or government-issued ID in a grocery store without being accused of using stolen finances?

34. Can you wait at a bus stop at noon without passers-by assuming that you are working in the survival sex trade?

35. If you are asked for proof-of-age in order to purchase tobacco or alcohol, can you be reasonably sure that the cashier is trying to prove your age, not your gender?

36. Can you be reasonably sure that, when dating someone new, they will be interested in getting to know your personality over and above your medical history?

37. Can you smile at a young child without their parents scorning or explaining you to the child?

38. Can you be sure that your gender identity doesn't automatically label you as an outsider, an anomaly, abnormal, or something to be feared?

39. Can you argue for gender equality without your right or motivation to do so being questioned?

40. Does the state of your genitals cause you to fear violence if they are discovered?

41. Are your height, weight, muscle mass, or hair follicles used as 'proof' that your gender identity is mistaken?

42. Are your height, weight, muscle mass, or hair follicles consistently pointed out as being incongruent with your gender?

43. Are your basic healthcare needs minimized by others who contrast them in priority with lifesaving surgeries?

44. Can you find a religious community that will not exclude you based upon your genital or hormonal structures?

45. If you are having a difficult time making new friends, can you generally be sure that it is not because of your gender identity?

46. Can you choose whether or not to think of your gender as a political or social construct?

47. When you tell people your name, do they ask you what your "real" name is?

48. Can you consider social, political, or professional advancements without having to consider whether or not your gender identity will be called into question as being appropriate for advancement?

49. Do people assume that they have a right to hear, and therefore ask, about your intimate medical history or future?

50. Can you find gendered privilege in other places?

Epilogue

Kate Bornstein and S. Bear Bergman

Kate Bornstein: So, what needs to develop is a politic of desire that matches our slippery identity of desire. People attacking you for being misogynist are flailing cruelly and thoughtlessly. They're operating on a politic of power, or a politic of identity at best.

KB: And I can see seeds of that politic in this book.

S. Bear Bergman: In many ways, art-wise and politics-wise, I feel like I started out drafting behind you. I got all these big ideas, and all this speed (not to mention a great view). Can I make a roller-derby metaphor? I feel like the one who gets flung forward by the most powerful grrl on the team.

KB: More than a politician, Bear, you're an artist and a visionary. You make a perfect target. I do kinda like the vision of you having me in tow, though. But that brings me back to visions of Sarah Palin and I know you don't want me to go on about that.

SBB: Please. I beg of you.

KB: Ah, me and Sarah. Swimming in the brisk, cold, sub-arctic waters of the Pacific Northwest, playing with the killer whales, holding each other's goose-pimpled bodies for warmth. Mmmmmm. What were you saying? Hang on, I'll read.

KB: Ah, me and Sarah Palin on a roller derby rink.

SBB: Careful. Extensive discussion of Clint Eastwood's willing asshole is only a few (key)strokes away.

KB: Does anyone fantasize about sex with Rush Limbaugh, do you think? Or Glenn Beck?

SBB: I imagine someone must. And I am sure that there are places all over the world where people ask one another the same horrified question about me. In fact, sometimes they ask it to my face.

KB: See? We need a Department of Looks & Abilities Studies.

SBB: We should volunteer to do their reader.

KB: Someone needs to write the first text as a single book. Someone who's reading this book probably will do exactly that.

KB: The thought of how this book is gonna ripple just tickles me pink.

SBB: I hope it does. I think it will. I wonder how much of it we'll even be able to see?

KB: Well, I saw a fuck of a lot more happen with this genderation of outlaws than I ever expected to see. My guess is you'll totally see blossoms out of this book. Me, maybe. I'll be in a rocking chair on some porch, and you'll nudge me and say "Hey, Kate. It worked. *Gender Outlaw: The Next Generation* is old already." And I'll look at you fondly and say, "Raisin Bran. I want me some Raisin Bran."

SBB: ::fond smile:: And I will fetch it.

KB: You, sir, are an amazing cool outlaw.

SBB: And you, most rockingest grrl, are my inspiration.

KB: Anon, then. Kiss kiss.

SBB: Big outlaw love.

We are five years old. Eighteen. Thirty-seven. Sixty. We are starting grad school, starting companies, starting families, and starting trends. We are serving coffee and signing paychecks, nursing the sick and teaching children, building technology, growing food, producing masterpieces, and changing laws. We are woven into this culture and we are finding each other. We are sharing our notes, strengthening our stories, reaching out for one another, and welcoming everyone in.

And when we wake up in five, ten, twenty-five years, we'll find that the queer issues we're fighting so hard for today have been trumped by an understanding of the fluidity of gender. We'll have learned that masculinity and femininity are not mutually exclusive, and how satisfying it can feel to represent both at once, or neither. We'll have learned that our genders—like our skills, our body types, and our parents' backgrounds—can be highly significant or completely irrelevant to our identities, depending on the situation. We'll know that our genders can mean different things at different times, and that they are not set in stone. We'll see them as just another set of colors that we can play with in our vibrant arsenals of finger paints.

We know this is already happening.

We are already here. We are already experimenting, expressing ourselves, facing our fears, and combating our shame. We are already asserting ourselves, creating spaces to play in, and giving others around us permission, by example, to join in.

And we are finding that we are further along than we imagined. There is less stopping us than we think.

—Sarah Dopp

About the Editors

KATE BORNSTEIN is an author, playwright, and performance artist whose work to date has been in service to sex positivity, gender anarchy, and building a coalition of those who live on cultural margins. Her work recently earned her an award from the Stonewall Democrats of New York City and two citations from New York City Council members.

Kate's books are taught in over 150 colleges around the world. Her latest book, *Hello, Cruel World: 101 Alternatives To Suicide For Teens, Freaks, and Other Outlaws*, was published in 2007. According to daily email and Twitter, the book is still helping people stay alive. Other published works include the books *Gender Outlaw: On Men, Women, and the Rest of Us* and *My Gender Workbook*. A new memoir, *Kate Bornstein Is A Queer and Pleasant Danger* is due out from Seven Stories Press in April 2011. Read more about Kate at www.katebornstein.com.

S. BEAR BERGMAN is the author of two books, most recently *The Nearest Exit May Be Behind You* (Arsenal Pulp, 2009), and four award-winning solo performances, and is a frequent contributor to anthologies on all manner of topics from the sacred to the extremely profane. A longtime activist, Bear was one of the founders of the first-ever Gay Straight Alliance, and has watched them spread with wonder. Ze continues to work at the points of intersection between and among gender, sexuality, and culture, and spends a lot of time trying to discourage people from installing traffic signals there. Bear lives in Toronto, Ontario with hir husband and son. Read more about Bear at www.sbearbergman.com.

About the Contributors

ROE-ANNE M. ALEXANDER is: a trannygirl, an underground comix artist, and an occasional burlesque performer. Current projects include: a zine about shamanism and a dictionary of fierce tranny comebacks. She plays guitar and sings in the Witch Chromosomes, a trannycore punk band. She is also the MC of Gendersmash, a monthly performance space and open mic for the gender variant community in Olympia, Washington. Feel free to check out her website, mothermarymorphine.tk, or contact her with any questions at rowannealexander@riseup.net.

MERCEDES ALLEN is a transgender advocate in Alberta, Canada who started AlbertaTrans.org as a network to help foster and support the Edmonton, Calgary, and rural communities within the province, as well as to provide information and training where requested. She has written for several group weblogs, including The Bilerico Project, PageOneQ, Pam's House Blend, Transadvocate, TransGroupBlog, Daily Kos, and others as well as her own Wordpress blog, DentedBlueMercedes. Her essay "Destigmatization Versus Coverage and Access: The Medical Model of Transsexuality" was also selected for inclusion in the forthcoming McGraw Hill text, *Taking Sides: Clashing Views in Human Sexuality.*

ZEV AL-WALID is a multilingual, Muslim, and queer. He has lived in Asia, Africa, North America, and Europe, and can't wait to explore the continents he's missed. A computer geek turned finance professional, he maintains a healthy disrespect for authority and a tendency to get his most productive work done late into the night.

A bi Jewish femme of color with a master's degree in Sexuality Studies, **A.P. ANDRE** writes extensively on sex, race, and gender. A.P. has essays in numerous books and lectures at schools and organizations across the country.

RYKA AOKI is a poet, performer, and composer whose work has been honored by the Academy of American Poets and the California State Senate. Ryka created Trans/Giving, LA's first art/performance series dedicated to trans, genderqueer, and intersex artists. Her current project is Office Hours, which matches trans-identified professors with trans-identified students entering or re-entering college. Ryka has a third-degree black belt in Kodokan Judo and is a professor of English at Santa Monica College.

AZADEH ARSANJANI will be my name before too much longer.

TAMIKO BEYER is a femme, cisgender queer woman. My work has appeared in *The Sonora Review, The Progressive, Gay and Lesbian Review, Cheers to Muses: Contemporary Work by Asian American Women*, and others. I was recently awarded a grant from the Astraea Foundation's Emerging Lesbian Writers Fund, and I am currently an M.F.A candidate at Washington University in St. Louis. I live in St. Louis during the school year, but my heart—and partner, and cats, and most of my books—are happily settled in Brooklyn.

JOHNNY BLAZES presents genre-bending, gender-blending performances infused with drag, burlesque, and circus arts while drawing from hir extensive background in classical voice, ballet, and theater. After spending several years directing grassroots circuses from Ohio to Massachusetts, with casts ranging in size from 12 to 95, Johnny has created a name for hirself as one of Boston's sassiest comedic cabaret artists.

AHIMSA TIMOTEO BODHRÁN is the author of *Antes y después del Bronx: Lenapehoking*, winner of the New American Press Chapbook Contest. His nonfiction and poetry appear in a hundred publications in fifteen nations. An activist and organizer, and American Studies Ph.D. candidate at Michigan State University, he is completing *Yerbabuena/Mala yerba, All My Roots Need Rain: mixed blood poetry & prose,* and *Heart of the Nation: Indigenous Womanisms, Queer People of Color, and Native Sovereignties*.

MICHA CÁRDENAS / AZDEL SLADE / dj lotu5 is a transgender artist, theorist and trickster. She will be a Lecturer in the Visual Arts department at UCSD in Fall and Winter of 2009. She is an Artist/Researcher in the Experimental Game Lab (experimentalgamelab.net) at CRCA and the b.a.n.g. lab at Calit2.net. Her interests include the interplay of technology, gender, sex, and biopolitics. She blogs at Transreal.org. Micha holds an MFA from the University of California San Diego, an MA in Media and Communications with distinction from the European Graduate School, and a BS in Computer Science from Florida International University. She has exhibited and performed in Los Angeles, San Diego, Tijuana, New York, San Francisco, Montreal, Egypt, Ecuador, Spain, and many other places. Micha has received grants from UCIRA, calit2, and Ars Virtua, and her work has been written about in publications including the *LA Times, San Diego Union Tribune, .dpi magazine,* and *Rolling Stone Italy*.

A memoirist and essayist by nature, **SHERILYN CONNELLY** has contributed to the anthologies *It's So You: 35 Women Write About Personal Expression Through Fashion and Style* by Seal Press; *I Do / I Don't: Queers on Marriage* by Suspect Thoughts Press; *Good Advice for Young Trendy People of All Ages* by Manic D Press; *More Five Minute Erotica* by Running Press; *Visible: A Femme-thology, Volume Two* by Homofactus Press; and periodicals such as *Girl-friends, Instant City*, and *Morbid Curiosity*. Much of her writing—including a daily diary maintained since 1999—can be found at sherilynconnelly.com, and she just completed a memoir entitled *Bottomfeeder*, the first in a planned trilogy. She also curates a weekly live comedy show called Bad Movie Night, because she considers it important to have fun on a regular basis.

ADRIAN DALTON is a gay transguy living in London with his cat, Elton. Prior to his transition he was very femme, did some modelling, and also tried to pass by becoming a faux queen (female bodied drag queen). He transitioned at the end of 2005 and is now trying to make a go of it as a drag queen, alter ego Lola Lypsinka. He also enjoys pole-dancing and writing.

KATIE DIAMOND is a radical queer comic artist and graphic designer. Art and politics are inextricably intertwined for Katie, as is evident in her numerous illustrations and cartoons about gender, sexuality, and sex education. Katie received a BFA from Maine College of Art, and has established herself in Portland, Maine as an artist-activist-advocate, doing everything from running Dr. Sketchy's Anti-Art School Burlesque Life Drawing Class and co-producing The Femme Show Portland to teaching art to disadvantaged youth and organizing a Voting Education and Registration Drive.

SARAH DOPP is obsessed with building websites and creating community spaces. She's the founder of Genderfork.com, a large community expression project about gender variance, and she's also the host of San Francisco's Queer Open Mic. You can find her in San Francisco or at SarahDopp.com.

FRANCISCO FERNÁNDEZ is an Argentinean kid who likes riding bikes, looking at pictures, and putting on airs of silliness. He's usually a queer trans boy, often genderqueer, and rarely sure. He's eighteen-years-old and hopes to start college soon.

STORMMIGUEL FLOREZ is a Mexican, a Maricon singer/songwriter, QueErotic performance artist, and live tranny sex show producer. Sometimes he does these things all at once. As a co-creator of Trans as Fuck and occasional leader of queer ritual, he is learning how to integrate trans and POC activism with sexiness and connection to Mama Earth.

My name is **JUDY WAWIRA GICHOYA** from Kenya. I am a twenty-year-old female student. I wrote this article with my friend and colleague **PRISCILLA MAINA** at Narok, Kenya. We are both final year medical students at the Moi University School of Medicine, due to graduate in November. I have always been interested in gender and sexuality studies and have attended fellowship training on the same. I hope in the future to work in this field, especially in providing quality and accessible health care to members of the LGBTI community.

LUIS GUTIERREZ-MOCK: a queer, biracial, transgender Chicano, Luis talks to his mother every day, goes to church on Sundays, works in HIV/AIDS prevention, and is totally in love with his fabulously well accessorized Chihuahua, FancyChuco Florez-Gutierrez-Mock. The creator of Mixed Fruit Productions, Luis produces events featuring multiracial queer performers and queer transracial adoptees. He holds a master's degree in Sexuality Studies from San Francisco State University, and he is completing his second master's degree, in Ethnic Studies. He is published in *Nobody Passes: Rejecting the Rules of Gender and Conformity*, co-authored *The Bay Area Multiracial Youth Resource Guide* with Dr. Andrew Jolivette, and is currently working on a research project in collaboration with Bay Area Young Positives, analyzing risk behaviors of young gay and bisexual multiracial men. He can be reached at luisgutierrezmock@yahoo.com.

JANET W. HARDY is a mass of seeming contradictions: mother and slut, dominatrix and homebody, intellectual and showtune queen. The author or coauthor of ten groundbreaking books about relationships and sexuality, including *The Ethical Slut* (75,000 copies sold to date, with a second edition recently published by Ten Speed Press), Janet has traveled the world as a speaker and teacher on topics ranging from ethical multipartner relationships to erotic spanking and beyond. She has appeared in documentary films, television shows, and more radio shows than she can count. Janet's writing has appeared in publications as various as *The Sondheim Review*, *Clamor*, and *EIDOS*. Her essay "Ex" was a finalist in the Event and New Letters creative nonfiction contests, and her article "When Love Trumps Gender: Gays and Lesbians in Opposite-Sex Relationships" was shortlisted for *Best Sex Writing 2008* from Cleis Press. She often fantasizes about being handcuffed to Stephen Sondheim's piano.

EVA HAYWARD is a guest researcher in Women's Studies at Duke University, and an assistant professor in the Department of Cinematic Arts, University of New Mexico. She has lectured and published widely on animal studies, experimental film, and embodiment. Her recently published essays, "Lessons From A Starfish: Prefixial Flesh and Transspeciated Selves" and "Spider City Self," explore intimacy, transsexuality, and animality.

simon iris hails currently from Portland, Maine, though is Philly born-and-bred. is a sexuality/sexual health educator working in HIV prevention, all the while floundering in academia and focusing his studies on American Sign Language. is hoping to eventually churn out a thesis regarding sexual consent in the d/Deaf community. is a taurus and pretty proud of it. is a musician that believes wholeheartedly in the benefits of public freelance art. is proud of continuing to survive four years of retail in order to do big important fun things. enjoys slam poetry, gender diversity, kink, listening to people talk, being extensively nerdy, making noise and breaking shit. will always believe in the inherent power of people to be and do amazing, beautiful things.

ANDREA JENKINS is a proud pre-op TG Woman of African American descent. Born in Chicago, Illinois, she has one daughter and one grand daughter. Her poetry and visual art reflects her committment to social activism and transgender equality. Andrea's work has appeared in *rock, paper, scissors; The International Journal of Transgenderism; Haute Dish;* and several journals. She is a prolific spoken word artist in Minneapolis and holds an MFA in Creative Writing from Hamline University.

ROZ KAVENEY is the author of various books on pop culture, a number of angry poems, and a vast fantasy epic, as yet unpublished but not like anything you have ever read. She first found the trans community when she was befriended by street whores in the grimy Manchester of the 60s and has been understanding her own and other people's transitions ever since, wandering through GLF, New Romantic bars, the dark streets of Chicago, and the company of academics. One day age may teach her wisdom, but not yet.

TELYN KUSALIK is a lovely person who you really should meet sometime. Ey was brought up in Halifax, Nova Scotia, and now lives in Montreal, Quebec, where ey has found a home—for now. Ey spends eir time making wonderful friendships, playing in an anarchist marching band, being a bit too much of a trans-activist, trying to find work as a teacher, going on long bike trips, and supporting the local queer and trans communities. Ey is proudly addicted to tea and cuddles. Ey wants to hear from all of you and can be reached at telyn.kusalik@gmail.com.

DANE KUTTLER's poetry is often lyrical and narrative, exploring themes of Jewish and queer identities, with a lot of love poems to her grandparents. The most common format for her work is the exploration of a relationship between two people that connects to broader political and social themes. She has featured in coffee shops, living rooms, libraries, back porches, and the occasional auditorium, but her favorite venue has always been her first—a dilapidated tree house with sixteen stuffed animals for an audience.

JOY LADIN, the David and Ruth Gottesman Professor at Stern College of Yeshiva University, is the first openly transgender employee of an Orthodox Jewish institution. She is the author of four books of poetry—*Psalms* (2010), *Transmigration* (2009), *The Book of Anna* (2006), and *Alternatives to History* (2003)—and her poems and essays have been widely published. Her essay is drawn from an unpublished collection of autobiographical reflections on transition from living as a man to living as a woman.

LEONA LO graduated from the University of York, United Kingdom, with Honors in English and Related Literature. Her autobiography was published by Select Books in 2003. Her one-woman *Ah Kua Show* was staged in Singapore in 2009. She is Principal Consultant of Talk Sense Pte Ltd and also the Founding Working Group member of the Asia Pacific Transgender Network.

SASSAFRAS LOWREY is a militant storyteller, artist, and educator who believes that everyone has a story to tell, and that the telling of those stories is essential to creating social change. Ze is the editor of the *Kicked Out* anthology and is a contributor to numerous anthologies. Sassafras lectures and performs for colleges and community groups across the country, and lives in New York City with hir partner, two puddle-shaped cats, and a princess dog. More information about Sassafras can be found at PoMoFreakshow.com.

BO LUENGSURASWAT is a Bangkok native who has called the Bay Area home since 2003. He is currently a graduate student in the Department of Asian American Studies at UCLA, where his research involves examining the experiences of Asian American and Asian immigrant FTMs through artistic and cultural production. Bo is also a practicing visual artist. His work was exhibited as part of *Fresh Meat in the Gallery* at the San Francisco LGBT Community Center in summer 2009.

KYLE LUKOFF grew up twenty miles north of Seattle and moved to New York City for college when he was eighteen. He currently resides in Brooklyn and is a writer, bookseller, and aspiring children's librarian. He generally identifies as a queer FTM, and will explain further if you ask him nicely.

QUINCE MOUNTAIN is an associate editor of *Killing the Buddha*, an online religion magazine for people made anxious by churches. He is currently at work on a book about sex change and evangelical Christianity.

SAM ORCHARD is a person who lives in Port Chalmers, Dunedin (a small grey town in the South Island of New Zealand), working as a youth worker and trying find time to sit with some paper and pencils. I draw stuff. It's fun. Oh yeh, I identify as trans, in some vague form—some queer conglomeration of parts that vaguely resemble a very feminine boy.

A former organizer, **cory schmanke parrish** works as a bookkeeper for the revolution, helping to keep New York City social justice organizations financially sound. parrish strives to write poems that are unflinchingly honest explorations of issues such as gender, white privilege, and our current political context, and also strives to make people laugh as often as possible.

SAM PETERSON is a Sam-of-all-trades. He's been a tattoo artist, a sex worker, and a travel agent; he's worked for glbt rights in Texas, taught feminist porn-writing cross country, and, of course, done a lot of performance art in between. Like you do. Sam hails from Austin, via Manhattan by way of D.C., and while his powers of observation were muddied there for a while, he saw it *all* and remembers most of it. He works in Chapel Hill, NC now, painting out of his home studio, writing incessantly for thamansam .blogspot.com and other projects, and cracking wise about the tragicomic pratfalls of being a middle-aged former woman with an eighteen-year-old boy's brain. He especially likes cephalopods and cats, but not together.

RAQUEL (LUCAS) PLATERO MÉNDEZ is a political activist and researcher at the Complutense University of Madrid, Spain. Since 2003 I have been involved in two European projects (MAGEEG and QUING), and my work relates to policy frames, intersectionality, intimate citizenship, and the entrance in the political agenda of LGBT issues in Spain. I am interested in the (ex)inclusion of sexual orientation and gender identity in gender equality policies; partnership rights and same-sex marriage and transgender rights along with the creation of public services for LGBT people; and the lesbian feminist discourses and their impact on gender equality policies. I am the co-author of two books: *Herramientas para combatir el Bullying Homofóbico* (*Tools to combat homophobic bullying*, Talasa, 2007) and *Lesbianas. Discursos y Representaciones* (*Lesbians. Discourses and Representations*, Melusina 2008).

RAFE POSEY used to be a suburban lesbian carpool mom. Now he's a city-dwelling transfag dad. He lives with a pack of rescued dogs and cats, far too many books, and the first woman to graduate from West Point. They share a passion for infrastructure, the Chesapeake Bay Watershed, and fine urban planning. Rafe is also an MFA student and adjunct professor of writing at the University of Baltimore.

AMIR RABIYAH lives in Oakland, California and is an Arab/queer/trans poet and performer. He received his BA in Women's Studies from Portland State University and his MFA in Writing and Consciousness from the New College of California. He has performed and read his poetry, fiction, and non-fiction all over the US and has been published in *Mizna, Riffrag, Tea Party Magazine* and the anthology: *I Saw My Ex at a Party*. He was a finalist in *Cutthroat Magazine*'s 2008 Joy Harjo Poetry Contest. This year, he was a featured writer with the Men's Story Project, a new performance and dialogue project exploring social ideas about masculinity. Amir is also a member of Mangos With Chili, a multi-racial, multi-gendered, and multi-genre traveling cabaret of queer and trans of color performance artists working in theater, dance, spoken word, burlesque, and drag.

ESMÉ RODRÍGUEZ (aka T. Kupin-Escobar) is a Queer, gender variant, Chicana, academic, artist, designer, and activist, originally from New York City and Morelos, Mexico. She has been performing in the Twin Cities of Minneapolis and St. Paul for ten years and has also traveled to be in drag shows both in San Francisco and Amsterdam, Holland. In "boi clothes, during the day," she is a Visiting Instructor of Hispanic Literatures and Gender Studies at Macalester College. She is currently ABD and working on her doctoral dissertation, which focuses on gender identities, performance studies, and the reconfiguration/deconstruction of femininities. The thesis, titled "Femininity: UN/STAGED," attempts to derive new and complex discourses surrounding the idea of multiple genders.

SCOTT TURNER SCHOFIELD is a man who was a woman, a lesbian turned straight guy who is often mistaken for a gay teenager. His three original solo performances, "Becoming a Man in 127 EASY Steps," "Debutante Balls," and "Underground Transit" have toured internationally since 2001. Scott is the recipient of several awards for his art, among them a "Fruitie" for Off-Broadway Performance, a Princess Grace Foundation Fellowship in Acting, and a Tanne Foundation Award for Commitment to Artistic Excellence. Scott's book, *Two Truths and a Lie* (Homofactus Press), was a finalist for two Lambda Literary Awards in 2008 and made the American Library Association's 2009 Rainbow List. He was also a finalist on ABC's *Conveyor Belt of Love*, along with a hardcore gay porn star and a naked man with a little dog. Scott's work tours in service of equal rights on the basis of gender identity and expression. To find out more, check out undergroundtransit.com.

JULIA SERANO is an Oakland, California-based writer, performer, and trans activist. She is the author of *Whipping Girl: A Transsexual Woman on*

Sexism and the Scapegoating of Femininity (Seal Press, 2007), a collection of personal essays that reveal how misogyny frames popular assumptions about femininity and shapes many of the myths and misconceptions people have about transsexual women. Julia's other writings have appeared in anthologies (including *BITCHfest: Ten Years of Cultural Criticism from the Pages of Bitch Magazine, Word Warriors: 30 Leaders in the Women's Spoken Word Movement* and *Yes Means Yes: Visions of Female Sexual Power and A World Without Rape*); in feminist, queer, pop culture, and literary magazines and websites (such as *Bitch, AlterNet.org, Out, Feministing .com, Clamor, Kitchen Sink, make/shift, other, LiP* and *Transgender Tapestry*); and have been used as teaching materials in gender studies, queer studies, psychology, and human sexuality courses in colleges across North America. For more information about all of her creative endeavors, check out juliaserano.com.

UZI SIOUX is a queer goth rollergirl who often wishes roller derby could be her full time job. She also occasionally wishes every day could be Halloween. She is an Environmentalist, a Feminist, and an LGBT activist. Her hobbies include studying academic theory, going to goth clubs, hiking, baking vegan pastries, and reading the poetry of Charlotte Mew.

CHRISTINE SMITH is a big ol' San Francisco Bay Area Transwoman with itchy drawing fingers and lots of characters in her head nagging her to let them out.

GWENDOLYN ANN SMITH is a writer, designer, and transgender activist in the San Francisco Bay Area. She is a pioneer in using cyberspace as a tool of activism, including the founding of the Remembering Our Dead web project and the Transgender Day of Remembrance. Gwen pens a regular column called "Transmissions" for the *Bay Area Reporter* and other newspapers. She shares her life with her partner of eighteen years, Bonnie.

EVIN TAYLOR is a Social Worker in Vancouver, British Columbia. He is a queer trans-man living happily with his very own tranny named Kimothy. Evin's passions include drug policy reform, social justice, tomato gardening, and all things whole wheat.

Born in Los Angeles in 1963, the person who would become **TAYLOR THORNE** was raised in accordance with having an outtie. A proud dropout of USC's Writing Program, she went on to pursue culinary arts. She moved to New Orleans to transition, where Hurricane Katrina was a major, though surmountable, setback. Presently, she is a successful caterer-chef and partnered to wonderful, gender blurry, Zan. They live in South Louisiana where one can actually be out as Trans.

KENJI TOKAWA was born, raised, and currently resides on Mississaugas of the New Credit territory; barely studies at the University of Toronto; and should make more phone calls home to Brampton. He is a writer, T-shirt maker, and grandson whose work has been published in *Culture-SHOCK! Queens University Anti-Racist Lit Review*, and his self-published chapbook entitled *Missing the Moon*. He recently had his poetry featured at Pride Toronto's 2009 Proud Voices Literary Stage. Kenji is also program co-ordinator of both the Toronto Asian Arts Freedom School and GenderFOC writing workshops for trans/gendervariant folks of color, co-investigator with the Trans PULSE project researching access to health care for trans people in Ontario, and workshop facilitator with the 519 Trans Access Project providing trans-positive training to service providers and students. He can be reached at kenji.tokawa@yahoo.ca.

PETERSON TOSCANO spent seventeen years and over $30,000 on three continents attempting to change and suppress his gay orientation and gender differences. This included two years at the notorious Love in Action ex-gay residential facility in Memphis, TN. Once he came out of the closet in 1998, he began to tell his story to others, and in 2003 he premiered a one-person comedy called *Doin' Time in the Homo No Mo Halfway House*. He has spoken out regularly in the media about the dangers of gay reparative therapy, and in 2007, along with fellow ex-gay survivor Christine Bakke, Peterson co-founded Beyond Ex-Gay (beyondexgay.com), a resource for ex-gay survivors. Peterson's theatrical performance pieces include *Queer 101—Now I Know My gAy,B,Cs, How the Indians Discovered Columbus*, and *The Re-Education of George W. Bush—No President Left Behind!* His most recent work is *Transfigurations—Transgressing Gender in the Bible*, a one-person play about transgender and gender-variant Bible characters. An obsessive blogger and a Quaker, Peterson's mission is to promote peace and reconciliation through storytelling—oh, and to find a decent vegan meal.

FRANCES VARIAN is a queer femme writer and activist currently living in Durham, North Carolina. Her journey toward overcoming late stage neurological and cardiac Lyme Disease can be found on-line at helphealfran.org. She dreams of being healthy enough to write for and travel to all of the beautiful queer people who make her joyful. She is grateful to be part of this amazing project and important conversation.

SHAWNA VIRAGO is a celebrated transgender songwriter and activist. Her music twists together punk roots rock and insurgent country, creating anthems for a new generation. The *SF Bay Times* said Miss Virago is a "transgender songwriting goddess who manages to channel Joe Strummer through a Candy Darling-like persona." She is the Director of Tranny

Fest, the nation's first transgender film festival. Her new album *Objectified* is available at shawnavirago.com.

SEAN SAIFA M WALL is an intersex man of African descent walking the lines of sobriety and gender. Hailing from the Boogie Down Bronx, Saifa currently resides in the Bay Area where he gardens, cooks, and explores new ways of eating, staying healthy, and living sustainably. Don't get it twisted though! He has a passion for music, writing, and bringing people together in community.

j wallace spends most of his time creating trouble for people who don't treat queer and trans people well. He does a great deal of this in schools, but doesn't stop there, with healthcare and government also being frequent targets. Professionally, he calls this training; personally he calls it very satisfying. j and his husband welcomed their first child this year, and are learning about what it means to parent their small son.

E.S. WEISBROT is a student, sex worker, writer, and performer who lives in Toronto, Ont. Currently working on her MSW degree, she is a feisty and outspoken advocate for trans and genderqueer communities. Her hope is to write and move and speak and create in ways that open people's minds to all the possibilities we fear and all those we have yet to discover.

CT WHITLEY was born and raised in Colorado. Although he has lived in the Virgin Islands, New York City, and Michigan, he considers the Front Range his home. An academic at heart, CT has a passion for research, focusing on social justice, environmental issues, animal welfare, and queer and trans studies. He is currently a PhD candidate in sociology.

Kate and Bear would like to thank:

Artists, Activists, Performers, and Simply Fabulous Stars Who Were Blazing Trails and Kickin' It Old School Before Most Anyone Else In Modern or Postmodern Trannydom:

Joan of Arc

The 3rd Earl of Southampton

Enrique Favez

Mary Frith (Moll Cutpurse)

Chevalier d'Eon de Beaumont

Lili Elbe

We'wha

Laurence Michael Dillon

Christine Jorgensen

Virginia Prince

The Jewel Box Revue

Stormé DeLarverie

Danny La Rue

April Ashley

Marlene Dietrich

Ed Wood

International Chrysis

Candy Darling

Jackie Curtis

Holly Woodlawn

Veronica Klaus

Miss Understood

Elvis Herselvis

Sylvia Rivera

Jan Morris

Wendy Carlos

Dr. Renée Richards

Caroline Cossey (aka Tula)

Dr. Sandy Stone

Marsha Botzer

Cheryl Chase

Zachary Nataf

Lou Sullivan

Doris Fish

'Tippi'

Miss X

Bob Davis

Canary Conn

Billy Tipton

The Cockettes

The Sisters of Perpetual Indulgence

Abe Rybeck

Rachel Pollack

Jill Enquist

Jason Cromwell

Chelsea Goodwin

Kim Christy

Miss Major

Christine Beatty

Jayne County

Jamison Green

David Harrison

David Bowie

Sophia Lamar

Grace Sterling Stowell

Bear Thunderfire

Jack O'Rion Barker

Wendy Chapkis

Miss Coco Peru

Bet Power

Dallas Denny

Davina Anne Gabriel

Quentin Crisp

Brandon Teena

Diana Montford

Charles Pierce

Charles Ludlam

Dr. Robert Lawrence

Dr. Carol Queen

Boy George

Lily Tomlin

Del LaGrace Volcano

Kristiene Clarke

Leslie Feinberg

Jacob Hale

Tony Barretto-Neto

Jennifer Miller

Diane Torr

Dr. Maxwell Anderson

Jason Elvis Barker

Shelley Mars

Pauline Park

Les Nichols

Charles Busch

Ethyl Eichelberger

Bette Bourne

John Epperson

Harvey Fierstein

The Lady Chablis

Nancy Nangeroni

Hal Fuller

Freddie Mercury

Norrie May-Wellby

Riki Wilchins

Patrick Califia

Rupert Raj

Susan Stryker

k.d. lang

Roz Kaveney

Stephen Whittle

Raven Kaldera

Divine

Kari Edwards

Spencer Bergstedt

Angela Taylor

Carson McGehee

Spike Harris

Wilson Cruz

Terri O'Connell

Alexis Dumont

Rosa von Praunheim

Lee J. Brewster

Billy DeFrank

Joann Roberts

Adèle Anderson

Martine Rothblatt

Michael Jackson

Maxwell Anderson

Angela Brightfeather

Jack Halberstam

Monica Roberts

Loren Rex Cameron

Dylan Scholinski

Anne Lawrence

Yoseñio Vicente Lewis

Dionne Stallworth

Anne Ogborn

Coccinelle

Lorraine Sade Baskerville

Lazlo Pearlman

Virginia Mollenkott

Jayne Thomas

Paisley Currah

Peggy Shaw

Joey Arias

Max Wolf Valerio

Dr. Marisa Richmond

Sherry Vine

Phranc

Marsha P. Johnson

Red Reddick

Red Dora

Robert Eads

Lola Cola

Michael Hernandez

Sky Renfro

Gwen Smith

Tyra Hunter

Kim Peirce

Imani Henry

Deirdre McCloskey

Christine Burns

Lady Bunny

Dean Spade

Theresa Sparks

Peaches Christ

Hedda Lettuce

Serge Nicholson

Eddie Izzard

Sile Singleton

Bibiana Fernández

Georgina Beyer

Lynnee Breedlove

RuPaul

Joan Roughgarden

Shannon Minter

Mara Keisling

Mr. Murray Hill

Dr. Marci Bowers

Mx. Justin Bond

We also thank:

The over three hundred more trans and trans-allied people who submitted work for this collection. Thank you for telling us your story, and please keep telling it to whomever you can whenever you can. We love the voices in this book, but there are already so many more voices!

All the early cyber-trannies from the AOL chat room, The Gazebo, and all the early gender "impostors" in the chat rooms of the 1990s.

All the nerd boys and nerd girls who were playing as non-gendered characters in the earliest online multi-user dungeon games.

All those who created the astonishingly elegant underground culture of clubs and societies: the middle-class straight white men who crossdressed in secret formality and the uptown black drag royalty who lived out in the street, and sometimes on the streets.

All the femmes and all the butches. Ever. All of 'em.

All the early trans activists from Stonewall to Ball Culture to the Imperial Court and The Transsexual Menace. And to every single drag queen from Sydney, Australia.

All the cross-dressed pantywaists, sissies, and mollies. And all the married men who wept alone at night wearing their wives' underclothes. All of our people who never could come out of some self-imposed, culturally-imposed, or morally imposed closet—no matter how good they were at passing.

All the cisgender actors and actresses who've done their best to play transgender people on stage and screen. They were all brave to do as much as they did.

All the utterly fabulous, fierce, and never-famous-enough female impersonators, female mimics, female illusionists, and femmophiles, as well as all the gender illusionists, drag kings, drag queens, she-males, he-shes, bulldaggers, and elegant swells, with special kisses to all the chicks with dicks and every single stone butch ever.

And we've been looking mostly at Euro-American cultures. Gotta shout out the two-spirits of native North America, hijras of India, fa'afafine of Samoa, onnagata of Japan, mahu of Hawaii, the kathoey of Thailand, travestis of Central and South America, and all the other ladyboys, dick girls, tomboys, wonder girls, effeminate men, masculine women, and trannies of any and all names from all around the globe.

Thank you for paving the way for us.

Bookwise, we also thank:

Malaga Baldi, agent of wonders, who managed all the many and myriad details of multinational contracts and all skabillion contributors with great patience and style.

Great magical heartfelt thanks to Brooke Warner at Seal, who gets credit for all the above-mentioned patience, plus her work and passion in pushing on both ends to make this book a reality.

Our contributors from around the world, who invited us to share their work and who were spectacularly good-natured about letting us pick exactly the bits that were right for this book.

And standing ovations to Zev Lowe, whose early editing assistance helped us see several diamonds in the rough (and whose general good nature made many tasks easier), and to Laura Waters Jackson, who took a graceful hand to the finished product and shined it up gorgeously.

With great love and respect,

Kate and Bear

Bear especially thanks, with a full heart and head-shaking wonder for what good care they all take of me:

My family of origin, especially my folks and my brother and sister-in-law, who have been on my side for a very, very long while.

My family of choice: Calvin Anderson, Joseph Berman, Hanne Blank, Steven Cohen, Malcolm Gin, Sasha T. Goldberg, Zev Lowe, Seth Marnin, Bobby Peck, Tori Paulman, and Scott Turner Schofield. Rockstars, all.

My husband, j wallace, who not only submitted a fantastic piece to our editorial eyes, but whose good cheer, support, and wise counsel got me through the process and who continues to be so spectacular that I seriously cannot believe my good fortune. Nevertheless, he sticks by me, loving me and amusing me with his mayonnaise imitation and making me sound smarter than I am. Lucky, lucky me.

And my co-editor, Kate Bornstein, longtime friend, treasured colleague, and cutest grrl I ever did see, whose smartypants thinking about gender is stupendous, and who inspires me to my shiniest butch self. Kate and I began exploring new ways of gender before I had any language to describe them, and she believed in me long before I believed in myself. I could not be gladder to finally be a big enough bear to start giving her a return on her investment.

Plus, Kate has this to say:

A loving bear hug to my co-editor S. Bear Bergman who opened all the doors, lit all the cigarettes, and did all the heavy lifting in the compilation of this book. Yes, yes, gentlemen are *supposed* to do those sorts of things, but Bear went above and beyond the call of gentlemanly duty and I am particularly thankful for his continued presence in my life.

Lastly, I thank my life partner Barbara Carrellas, whose research and discoveries in the field of sacred sex and gender-free orgasms provide body-level grounding to the theory that there might be more than two genders. After decades of theory, it's a lovely thing to scream with joy at the proof.